Introduction

Earthquakes and Volcanoes is an exciting, whole-language thematic unit. These 80 pages were designed to immerse children in language arts, science, math, social studies, and art. The literature and activities used in this thematic unit are sure to interest and motivate your students. A variety of teaching strategies such as cooperative learning, hands-on experiences, and child-centered assessment are integrated throughout. This literature-based thematic unit has two high-quality selections at its core: *Earthquakes* by Seymour Simon and *Volcano: The Eruption and Healing of Mount St. Helens* by Patricia Lauber.

This thematic unit includes the following:

❏ **literature selections**—summaries of two books with related lessons (complete with reproducible pages) that cross the curriculum

❏ **planning guides**—suggestions for sequencing the lessons for each day of the unit

❏ **bulletin board ideas**—suggestions and plans for student-created and/or interactive bulletin boards

❏ **curriculum connections**—in language arts, math, science, social studies, and art

❏ **a culminating activity**—which requires each student to synthesize his or her learning to produce a product or engage in an activity

❏ **an answer key**—provides answers for many of the student activities in this unit

❏ **a bibliography**—suggested additional fiction and nonfiction books related to the theme

> To keep this valuable resource intact so that it can be used year after year, you may wish to punch holes in the pages and store them in a three-ring binder.

Introduction (cont.)

Why a Balanced Approach?

The strength of a whole-language approach is that it involves children in using all modes of communication—reading, writing, listening, observing, illustrating, speaking, and doing. Communication skills are interconnected and integrated into lessons that emphasize the whole of language. Balancing this approach is our knowledge that every whole—including individual words—is composed of parts and directed study of those parts can help a student to master the whole. Experience and research tell us that regular attention to phonics, other word-attack skills, spelling, etc., develops reading mastery, thereby completing the unity of the whole-language experience. The child is thus led to read, write, spell, speak, listen, and think confidently in response to a literature experience introduced by the teacher. In these ways, language skills grow rapidly, stimulated by direct practice, involvement, and interest in the topic at hand.

Why Thematic Planning?

One very useful tool for implementing a balanced language program is thematic planning. By choosing a theme with correlating literature selections for a unit of study, a teacher can plan activities throughout the day that lead to a cohesive, in-depth study of the topic. Students will be practicing and applying their skills in meaningful contexts. Consequently, they will tend to learn and retain more. Both teachers and students will be freed from a day that is broken into unrelated segments of isolated drill and practice.

Why Cooperative Learning?

Besides academic skills and content, students need to learn social skills. This area of development cannot be taken for granted. Students must learn to work cooperatively in groups in order to function well in modern society. Group activities should be a regular part of school life, and teachers should consciously include social objectives as well as academic objectives in their planning. For example, a group working together to solve a problem may need to select a leader. In this case, the teacher should make clear to the students the qualities of good leader-follower group interaction just as they would state and monitor the academic goals of the project.

Four Basic Components of Cooperative Learning

1. In cooperative learning all group members need to work together to accomplish the task.

2. Cooperative learning groups should be heterogeneous.

3. Cooperative learning activities need to be designed so that each student contributes to the group, and individual group members can be assessed on their performance.

4. Cooperative learning teams need to know the academic and social objectives of a lesson.

THEMATIC UNIT
Earthquakes and Volcanoes

Written by Diann Culver

Teacher Created Resources, Inc.
6421 Industry Way
Westminster, CA 92683
www.teachercreated.com
ISBN: 978-1-57690-591-3
©2000 Teacher Created Resources, Inc.
Reprinted, 2012
Made in U.S.A.

Edited by
Mary Kay Taggart

Illustrator
Chandler Sinnott

Cover Art by
Larry Bauer

Table of Contents

Earthquakes

by Seymour Simon
Summary

Earthquakes can strike anywhere and at any time. Seymour Simon's *Earthquakes* describes earthquakes by using engaging text and startling photographs of actual earthquake damage. This book includes facts about the frequency of earthquakes in certain areas, fault lines, plate tectonics, and the measurement of earthquakes. It gives many examples and accompanying photographs. The book concludes by giving some safety measures to use during earthquakes.

The outline below is a suggested plan for using the various activities that are presented in this unit. You should adapt these ideas to fit your classroom situation.

Note: Use Section by Section (pages 7–12) as a discussion guide for Lessons 1–5.

Sample Plan

Lesson 1

- Read and discuss pages 1–6.
- Complete the Fault Lines activity (page 13).
- Complete Swirling Currents (page 14).

Lesson 2

- Read and discuss pages 7–10.
- Do the Plate Tectonics activity (page 15).
- Complete Earth's Jigsaw Puzzle (pages 16 and 17) and Salt Sculptures (pages 64 and 65).
- Demonstrate the layers of Earth with the Food for Thought activity (pages 18 and 19).

Lesson 3

- Read and discuss pages 11–14.
- Complete the math activity, Predicting Earthquakes (pages 47–49).

- Make a Model of Earth (pages 66 and 67).

Lesson 4

- Read and discuss pages 15–20.
- Do the Seismic Waves experiment (page 20).
- Read and discuss pages 21–26.

Lesson 5

- Read and discuss pages 27–29.
- Complete Earthquake Engineers (page 21).
- Complete Earthquake Safety (page 22).
- Conclude this portion of the unit with Earthquake Legends (pages 41 and 42).
- Assign other Across the Curriculum activities throughout this unit as you choose.

Overview of Activities

Setting the Stage

1. Create a map of the United States that shows the regions that are at the greatest risk for earthquakes. Use page 8 of *Earthquakes* as a guide. Display the map on a bulletin board during the earthquake part of this unit. Have the students note the amount of risk in living in their community. Discuss.

2. Ask the students about their personal experiences with earthquakes. Discuss some recent and major earthquakes that have been in the news.

Enjoying the Book

1. It is recommended that the book be divided into short segments for better understanding of the concepts. A summary of suggested segments and discussion information is given in Section by Section (pages 7–12).

2. Use the Fault Lines (page 13) demonstration to show the students how cracks in Earth's crust cause earthquakes.

3. Complete the Swirling Currents experiment on page 14 to demonstrate the swirling convection currents in Earth's mantle. This activity will also show how the movement plays a part in earthquakes.

4. The Plate Tectonics activity (page 15) will give the students hands-on experience with how plate tectonics and fault lines work together to cause earthquakes.

5. Allow the students to discover how the present-day continents can fit together like puzzle pieces to form the super continent Pangaea. This activity, Earth's Jigsaw Puzzle, is on pages 16 and 17.

6. Increase the students' understanding of how the land areas of Pangaea broke up by making Salt Sculptures (pages 64 and 65).

7. In the Food for Thought activity (pages 18 and 19) the students will compare and contrast cross sections of apples to Earth and its layers. As an extension the students, within cooperative groups, will compare oranges to Earth.

8. The Predicting Earthquakes lesson (pages 47–49) will require the students to use their math skills to study the occurrence of earthquakes along California's San Andreas Fault.

9. The students will better understand Earth's inner and outer layers after doing the Model of Earth activity on pages 66 and 67.

10. In the Seismic Waves experiments use a Slinky®, a rope, blocks, balls, and water to learn how seismic waves travel through the earth. Directions for these experiments can be found on page 20.

11. Discuss the necessity to build structures that can withstand powerful earthquakes. Follow up the discussion using the Earthquake Engineers activity on page 21.

12. Ask the students to complete the Earthquake Safety questionnaire (page 22). Discuss their answers and go over some basic safety tips if an earthquake were to strike.

Extending the Book

1. Use Earthquake Legends on pages 41 and 42 to share with the students some of the legends about the sources of earthquakes. Discuss the geographical origins of these legends. Challenge the students to create their own legends.

2. As a class develop a booklet or brochure for parents and students outside of the class, containing information on earthquakes in the area. Include probability statistics for the area, how to prepare for an earthquake, and how to stay safe if one should occur.

Section by Section

Earthquakes was written by the award-winning science author Seymour Simon. The stunning photographs and color illustrations along with the descriptive text will help students understand what causes earthquakes, how they are measured, and the resulting devastation that can follow. The book can be divided into short sections, read, and discussed as a group. Then section-specific activities can be done as reinforcement. The following summary can be used as a discussion tool so that the students reap the greatest benefit from the book. Special attention should be directed toward the information that will be needed to complete the activities following each section.

Pages 1–6

What Makes the Earth Shake?

An earthquake is the sudden trembling, shaking, and rolling of the earth's surface. An earthquake occurs when two parts of the earth's lithosphere slide sideways, away from each other, or into each other. Most earthquakes originate along plate boundaries called seismic activity or earthquake regions, at convergent and subduction zones. A *convergent zone* is an area along plate edges where one plate slips along the boundary of another plate. A *subduction zone* is an area where one plate slides down under or is thrust up over another plate. Plates can *converge* or move toward each other, *diverge* or pull away from each other, or slide sideways in a *lateral* movement. Any sudden plate movement causes an earthquake.

Earthquakes sometimes split the ground apart along a line called a fault. A *fault* is a crack or scar in Earth's crust. There are three types of faults. On a *dip-slip fault* line, rocks are pulled apart in an up and down movement. On a *strike-slip fault* line, rocks slide apart. Rocks are crushed together on a *reverse fault* line.

Pages 7–10

Earthquake Zones Plate Tectonics

The study of earthquakes is called *seismology*. Scientists who study earthquakes are called *seismologists*. Scientific theory or understanding of how plates move is called *plate tectonics*.

Scientists believe that Earth was formed about five billion years ago as a fiery, hot planet. Earthquakes shook the ground causing volcanoes to erupt constantly. Blistering hot gases, water vapor, and molten lava burst from volcano vents. Violent storms of acid rain raged, filling the early oceans.

Over millions of years, the air and water cleared and the earth cooled. The cooler temperatures caused Earth's crust to crack like an eggshell. It split into seven large and 12 small pieces. The large pieces formed the seven continents of North America, South America, Europe, Asia, Africa, Australia, and Antarctica.

Section by Section *(cont.)*

Pages 7–10 *(cont.)*

These pieces, called *plates*, float on hot convection currents in Earth's mantle where extreme heat from Earth's core has turned solid rock into a thick liquid called *magma*. The swirling magma currents constantly move the plates, pushing some together and pulling others apart. Where the plates move apart, magma rises up, spills out onto the ocean floor, cools, and forms new land. Magma also can push through the cracks in Earth's crust and erupt out as volcanic lava. The pushing together of plates formed the great mountain ranges of the world.

Since Earth's beginning, it has been in a state of constant change. Two hundred million years ago Earth was one massive supercontinent called *Pangaea* (derived from *pan* which means all, and *gia* which means Earth), and one enormous ocean called *Panthalassa* (*thalassa* means sea). Scientists believe that the supercontinent Pangaea began to break up 225 million years ago along what is now the mid-Atlantic ocean ridge. The lands we now live on have slowly drifted around Earth for millions of years and continue to move today about 2" (5 cm) per year. If the land masses could be pushed together, the pieces would fit like a huge jigsaw puzzle.

Some scientists believe that the separation of the supercontinent reverses and repeats itself every 440 million years. They believe that the continents split and drift apart for 200 million years, then reverse and drift back together again. If this is true, it is believed that the cycle of drifting apart is almost over, and the continents will soon begin to drift back together, eventually reforming a supercontinent again.

Earthquake Zones

Earthquake or seismic activity zones are all over the world. There are two primary bands of earthquake activity. The first is the *circum-pacific belt* that rings the coast of the Pacific Ocean (sometimes referred to as the *Ring of Fire*). The second is the *alpide belt*, along the southern boundary of the Eurasian Plate that cuts from the Atlantic Ocean across the Mediterranean into Asia. On the map on page 9 of *Earthquakes*, the red dots illustrate the number of earthquakes that have taken place along these plate boundaries in comparison to earthquakes in other parts of the world.

Understanding the Earth

Earth is not a perfectly round sphere but is rather more egg-shaped. It is made up of five important layers: the atmosphere, the hydrosphere, the lithosphere, the mantle, and the core. The lithosphere, mantle, and core are divided into several smaller parts. The atmosphere is made of gases. The hydrosphere is liquid. The core, mantle, and lithosphere are mostly solid.

The *atmosphere* contains many kinds of gases that support life and protect it from harmful radiation caused by the sun. It is about 700 miles (1,120 km) thick. It is made up of 78% nitrogen, 21% oxygen, and a 1% mixture of other gases including carbon dioxide. Oxygen, the gas that humans need to stay alive, makes up only 21% of Earth's atmosphere.

The *hydrosphere* is a layer of water that includes oceans, lakes, rivers, inland seas, underground waters, and all other water surfaces. The hydrosphere covers 70% of Earth's surface.

Section by Section *(cont.)*

════════════════════════ **Pages 7–10** *(cont.)* ════════════════════════

The *lithosphere* includes the crust and the upper mantle and extends 60 miles (96 km) deep into Earth. The lithosphere is made up of many rocky mineral compounds including oxygen, silicon, aluminum, iron, calcium, sodium, potassium, magnesium, and titanium.

The *crust* is divided into two parts. The upper or *sialic crust*, consisting of the seven continents, is made up of igneous and sedimentary rocks similar to granite. The lower or *simatic crust*, consisting of the ocean floor, is made up of heavy igneous rock and basalt. Earth's crust is thicker under the continents, about 19 miles (30 km) deep, and thinner under the oceans, about 3 miles (5 km) deep.

A thin layer of seismic activity called the *Moho Discontinuity*, which is responsible for breaking up earthquake waves as they pass through it, lies just below the crust. This Moho zone separates the upper mantle and Earth's crust.

The *mantle* is a shell of thick, melted rock that surrounds Earth's core. It is divided into two parts called the upper mantle and lower mantle. The mantle is about 1,800 miles (2,880 km) thick, extending from just below Earth's crust to just above the core. The mantle is composed of magnesium, silicon, and iron. A zone of weakness, called the *asthenosphere*, separates the upper mantle from the lower mantle.

Earth's tectonic plates (seven large and twelve small) float on the partially melted rocks of the asthenosphere. Extreme heat from the core continually pushes upward through the mantle, causing thick currents of swirling liquid rock and gases called *magma*. These *convection currents* are the force behind continental drift that caused the breakup of Pangaea. They also supply the rock for mid-ocean ridges and the fiery hot lava that erupts from volcanoes all over the earth.

Earth's inner core and outer core have a combined radius of about 2,175 miles (3,480 km). The *core* is made of metallic iron and nickel and is divided into two parts. The inner core is solid and extremely hot with temperatures from 4,982–6,649° F (9,000–12,000° C). The inner core's intense temperatures cause the outer core to melt slightly, forming an almost liquid, molasses-like mass with valleys and peaks where hot material has pushed upward.

════════════════════════ **Pages 11–14** ════════════════════════

San Andreas Fault

The San Andreas Fault lies on the Pacific coastline of the United States within one of the primary earthquake zones. The fault is a lateral or transform fault that is a part of what is known as the Ring of Fire where earthquakes occur more frequently. It is the boundary between the North American and Pacific tectonic plates. Most faults are located below the ocean, but the San Andreas Fault traverses into California for hundreds of miles. Scientists believe that the 600 miles (960 km) long San Andreas Fault is about 29 million years old. Rock formations show that it has slipped northwesternly approximately 350 miles (560 km) in the last 10 million years. Both sides of the fault appear to have moved to the right in what is known as a *right-lateral strike-slip*. The land moves slowly, about 2" (50 cm) per year, most of the time, but sometimes the land slips suddenly, causing an earthquake.

Section by Section *(cont.)*

Pages 15–20

Measuring Earthquakes

The point where an earthquake originates is called the focus or *hypocenter*. The *epicenter* is the point on Earth's surface directly above the focus. *Seismic* or *earthquake waves* create circular, expanding waves that radiate through the earth from the focus. The *primary* or *pressure waves (P-waves)*, somewhat like sound waves, are very fast. They travel through rock and soil at speeds of 3.8 miles (6 km) per second and through water at a slower speed of about 1.2 miles (2 km) per second. Primary waves jolt and shake the ground. *Secondary* or *shear waves (S-waves)* travel only through solids at about 1.9 miles (3 km) per second. Secondary waves produce a twisting and turning motion.

The motions of all waves are characterized by three things. The time period between the beginning and end of a wave vibration is called *Period (T)*. The magnitude of the wave's vibration is called *amplitude A*. The number of wave vibrations per second is called *frequency (F)*. Earthquakes are recorded by an instrument called a *seismograph*. Seismographs record the period (T), frequency (F), and amplitude (A) of the earthquake wave.

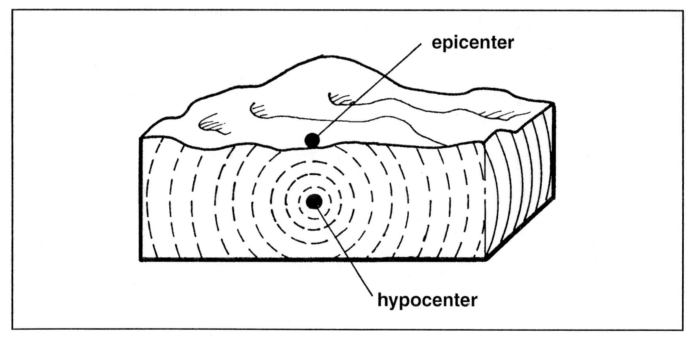

When the waves reach the earth's surface, they change to surface waves. *Love waves* travel quickly, with parallel and vertical shearing motions, causing the ground to tremble and shake. *Raleigh waves* travel more slowly but are more dangerous because they cause the earth to bend and twist.

The magnitude of an earthquake is measured by using a *Richter Scale*. The Richter scale measures the amount of energy released during an earthquake. The scale has a range from 1 for low energy to 10 for high energy. A reading of 2 is 30 times stronger than a reading of 1. An earthquake that measures a magnitude 5 or 6 is considered a low intensity earthquake. One that measures a magnitude of 7 is considered a medium intensity. And one that measures a magnitude of 8 or above is considered strong. The strongest earthquakes, however, are not necessarily the most deadly. A low intensity earthquake that occurs in a heavily populated area is extremely destructive, and the fires that may follow earthquakes can cause massive damage and many lost lives.

Section by Section *(cont.)*

━━━━━━━━━━━━━━━━━━━━ **Pages 21–26** ━━━━━━━━━━━━━━━━━━━━

Tsunami (*soo-NAH-mee*)

A *tsunami* is a huge wave caused when the level of the sea drops suddenly because of an earthquake, volcanic eruption, or a landslide along tectonic plate boundaries in the ocean. Ocean water pours quickly into the hole created by the dropped sea floor. When the hole is filled, the water retreats as a wave. The disturbance creates a series of waves much like ripples that develop when a rock is thrown into a pool of water. When the wave begins in the open sea it travels very fast and is usually only about 1 foot high (31 cm). However, as it reaches the shore, the wave slows down and builds into a huge wall of water that can be 100 feet (31 m) high. A tsunami usually comes ashore in eight or nine waves from 15 minutes to an hour apart. It can travel thousands of miles from its origin and can crash into land traveling at 400 miles (640 km) per hour.

Because of a tsunami's great size and speed, it can travel many miles inland and have the destructive force of several million tons of dynamite. Most of the time people have several hours warning, but sometimes there is very little time to prepare.

━━━━━━━━━━━━━━━━━━━━ **Pages 27–29** ━━━━━━━━━━━━━━━━━━━━

What Happens in an Earthquake?

The first sign of an earthquake is usually when the ground trembles and shakes and a loud sound somewhat like thunder, caused by movement of the air, can be heard. As seismic waves move through the earth, land rises and then falls again. Cement highways and railroad tracks rise up, buckle, twist, and break. Homes and other structures shake apart and crumble. Power and telephone lines break. Water and sewer pipes snap and burst open. Explosive fires start when gas lines are ruptured. The earth splits open and swallows everything above the crack. Mountains can be split in half and ice slides down the sides as an avalanche. In a few seconds, an earthquake reduces everything in its path to rubble causing loss of many lives and millions of dollars in property damage.

Building in Earthquake Zones

Years ago when an earthquake occurred people took cover and hoped for the best. Now new buildings in earthquake zones are built to withstand some of the force and are a lot safer. Although no building is earthquake proof, modern buildings are made to move up and down or back and forth without major damage. Buildings are also built on a base of rock, where buildings do not shake as hard.

Architects know that seismic waves passing through soft sand or loose soil will destroy anything that sits on top of it. They also know that brick houses that are reinforced with steel and well-built wood-frame houses can bend as the earthquake waves strike them. Tall buildings that are designed to sway like trees, buildings set on rollers, shock absorbers or isolators, and foundation support structures, all help to keep buildings safe in earthquakes.

Section by Section *(cont.)*

━━━━━━━━━━━━━━━━━━━━━━ **Pages 27–29** *(cont.)* ━━━━━━━━━━━━━━━━━━━━━━

Protection in an Earthquake

Earthquakes can happen anywhere. Just because an area is not in an earthquake zone does not mean that it is absolutely safe. Most injuries in an earthquake are due to falls, being thrown into or bumping into other objects, and being hit by falling objects. Structural collapse contributes to only 2% of the injuries and deaths. Based on the above, it is best to stay inside a building. Get under a strong table or desk and remain there until the quake is over. If there is nothing to get under, crouch down close to an inside corner wall and cover your head. Stay away from windows that can shatter and send shards of glass into the room. If you are caught in the car when an earthquake hits, move to the shoulder, staying away from power lines, and stay in your car until it's over.

Earthquake Folklore

Ancient legends from all over the world have attributed earthquakes to animals. The ancient Chinese believed that a winged dragon-snake shook the earth. Snakes also appeared in legends from Chile and medieval Italy. In India people believed that a giant elephant caused the tremors.

Unusual behavior as a predictor of earthquakes is a popular theory. According to witnesses the following phenomena have been observed before earthquakes:

- animals become nervous
- dogs howl for days
- cats run away
- birds fly in circles
- roosters fly to the tops of trees
- wild animals behave as if they are tame
- snakes and bears come out of hibernation
- mice stop and freeze in fear
- lakes become muddy
- lights appear in the sky
- air becomes unusually hot and dry
- flowers bloom in the winter
- birds and butterflies migrate hundreds of miles and return to the exact place of their birth by using their sensitivity to the earth's magnetic field or the polarization of the sun's light

Many animals possess senses more refined than those of humans, so it is not hard to believe that they may be more sensitive to changes deep within the earth.

Fault Lines

Materials

- two wooden blocks approximately 2" x 6" x 12" (5 cm x 15 cm x 31 cm)
- 10–15 small wooden or plastic cubes
- enlarged pictures of faults (see below)

Procedure

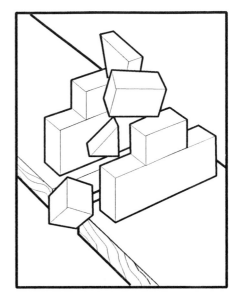

Place the two wooden blocks end-to-end. Use the small cubes to build a structure (somewhat like a building) on top of the blocks. Center the structure so that it is over the seam where the blocks meet. Explain to the students that the seam of the two blocks represents a fault line and that when an earthquake occurs, a fault or crack in the earth's crust can pull apart, slide sideways, or push up and down. Ask the students to observe as you demonstrate a dip-slip, strike-slip, and reverse faults to show what can happen when structures are built on top of or close to faults.

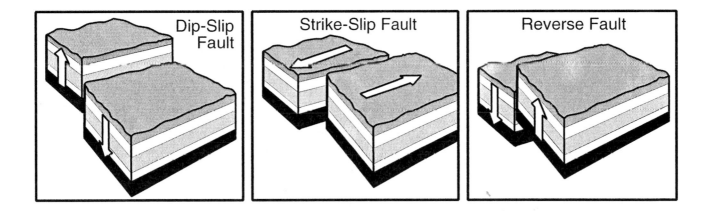

Dip-Slip Fault   Strike-Slip Fault   Reverse Fault

Fundamental Facts

Faults are huge cracks in Earth's crust. Fault lines may extend over 600 miles (960 km) along a crack. Once the ground breaks, it is always weaker in that area. As these weak areas are pushed together or pulled apart, pressure builds up and finally is released in the form of an earthquake. Fault lines are primary earthquake zones.

Swirling Currents

Materials

- small glass bottle (hot/cold resistant)
- large glass jar with a wide mouth (hot/cold resistant)
- red food coloring
- tongs
- funnel
- cold water
- boiling water

Procedure

Fill the large jar ¾ full with cold water. Fill the small jar ¾ full with boiling water. Add a few drops of red food coloring to the water in the small jar. Use the tongs to lift the small jar and carefully lower it into the cold water. Gently set it on the bottom of the large jar. Allow the students to watch the reaction that takes place. Ask open-ended questions about the demonstration and encourage the students to respond. Use the "Fundamental Facts" section below to explain the reaction.

Fundamental Facts

Hot water is lighter than cold water and therefore rises upward. As it cools it becomes heavier and begins to sink. This same process happens to magma in Earth's mantle. The magma becomes lighter and rises. When it gets closer to the crust, it begins to cool and sink again. The process creates the convection currents that constantly move and swirl. Earth's tectonic plates ride like giant rafts on top of the swirling convection currents.

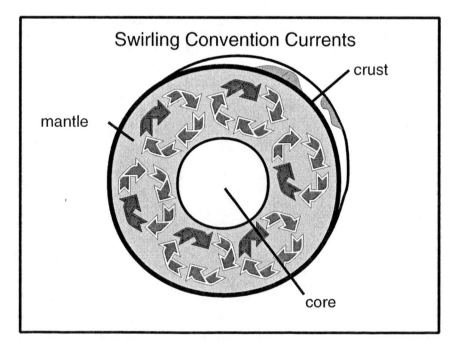

Swirling Convention Currents

mantle

crust

core

Plate Tectonics

Materials

- peanut brittle or similar hard candy
- white paper

Procedure

Give each student a piece of white paper and a piece of candy that is large enough to break into two pieces. Tell them to pretend that the candy represents Earth's crust and as it cools it breaks into large pieces. Allow a few students at a time to break the candy in half until everyone has snapped their candy in half. Now have the students each lay the candy on the white paper and fit it back together as tightly as possible. Explain that Earth's tectonic plates fit together in much the same way. Have the students experiment with the candy, strongly pushing and sliding it along the crack lines.

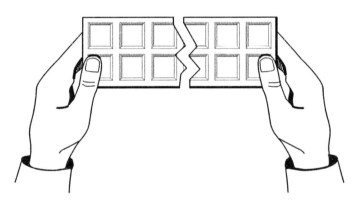

Fundamental Facts

Earth began as a fiery hot planet. After millions of years, the earth cooled, and the cooler temperatures caused the crust to crack like an eggshell. It split into seven large and twelve small pieces. The large pieces formed the seven continents of North America, South America, Europe, Asia, Africa, Australia, and Antarctica.

These pieces, called tectonic plates, float on Earth's mantle where extreme heat from Earth's core has turned solid rock into a thick liquid called magma. The swirling convection currents of red-hot magma constantly force the plates together or pull them apart. Finally, they slide sideways, under, or over another plate causing an earthquake.

Earth's Jigsaw Puzzle

Materials

- World Puzzle Pieces (page 17)
- crayons
- scissors
- glue
- blue construction paper

Procedure

Enlarge the World Puzzle Pieces (page 17) for each student. Have the students color the pieces different colors, carefully cut out the seven pieces, fit them together like a puzzle, and glue them onto blue construction paper. Ask them to entitle their work "Earth's Jigsaw Puzzle."

Variation

Divide the students into small groups. Enlarge the puzzle pieces and give a set to each group. Tell the groups to arrange their pieces onto blue poster board and glue them in place. Ask the groups to share their results.

Pangaea

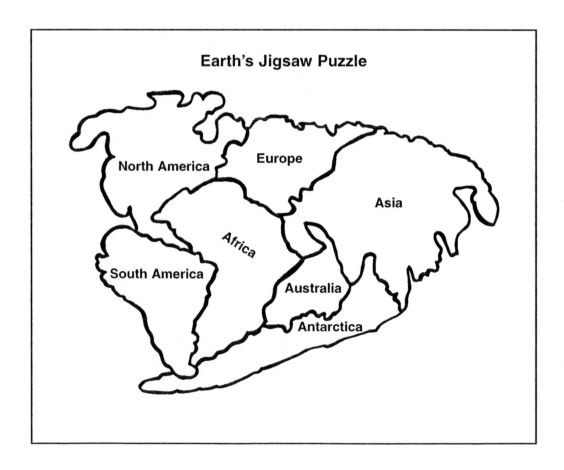

Earth's Jigsaw Puzzle

Earth's Jigsaw Puzzle *(cont.)*

World Puzzle Pieces

Directions: Cut out the pieces to the puzzle and glue them onto blue construction paper to construct the super continent, Pangaea.

Food for Thought

Apple Model

Materials

- three apples
- a sharp knife
- a cutting board
- paper towels

Procedure

Before beginning this demonstration, ask the students the following questions. Write down their responses or draw their interpretations on a chart.

"What is on the outside Earth?"

"What is inside Earth?"

"What is on the outside of an apple?"

"What is inside an apple?"

Cut one apple in half vertically and a second apple in half horizontally. Ask, "How are these apples like Earth?" and again chart students' answers.

Continue the demonstration by cutting a one-quarter section out of the third apple. Discuss the different appearances of the fruit when it is cut in half vertically, cut in half horizontally, and cut with a quarter removed.

Explain that the same thing can look different when seen from different angles or from different points or places.

Fundamental Facts

Explain that scientists have never seen the inside Earth, but they believe that it is composed of many layers. They say that the center of Earth is made up of an inner and outer core, and the area surrounding the core is called the mantle. The part that we live on is called the crust. The crust is very thin in relation to the mantle, just as the apple skin is thin in relation to the apple's fruit. The apple's skin represents Earth's crust. The fruit of the apple represents Earth's mantle layer. The apple's core and center represent Earth's inner and outer core.

Extension

Have the students answer the question, "How is an apple like Earth?" as a writing activity. They may also draw Earth and an apple and label the parts to show the comparison through illustrations.

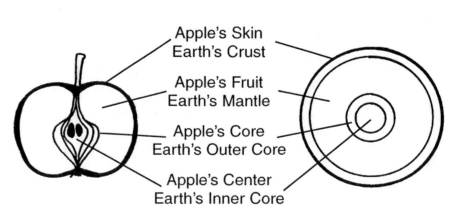

Apple's Skin
Earth's Crust

Apple's Fruit
Earth's Mantle

Apple's Core
Earth's Outer Core

Apple's Center
Earth's Inner Core

Food for Thought *(cont.)*

Orange Model

Materials

- oranges
- a knife
- rubber bands
- a cutting board
- paper
- paper towels
- pencils

Preparation

Divide the students into groups of four for this cooperative learning activity. Cut an orange into four equal sections for each group. Reassemble each orange and hold it together with a rubber band. Give a banded orange, paper towels, a piece of paper, pencils, and a copy of the information and questions below to each group.

Procedure

Read the Fundamental Facts, follow the directions below, and then answer the questions at the bottom of the page on a separate piece of paper. All group members should agree on the answers and sign the paper.

Fundamental Facts

A long time ago people believed that Earth was flat and that you could fall off if you got too close to the edge. In reality Earth has a round or spherical shape. Because we live on a small section of Earth, we cannot see its true shape. Astronauts were the first to actually see the true shape of Earth when they traveled into space. On Earth you can see the round shape of the horizon at an ocean or desert. Earth has four distinct layers: the inner core, outer core, mantle, and crust. The outer layer, called the crust, is divided into two parts. The seven continents sit on the upper or sialic crust. The floor of the ocean is considered the lower or simatic crust.

Directions

Read the questions below before beginning the project. Look closely at the shape of the orange before taking off the rubber band. Take the rubber band off of the orange. Give one section to each group member. Examine the surface of the cut sections. Tear the fruit away from the orange peel. Look at its flatness. Pull away some of the white membrane from under the peel layer. Answer the questions below.

Questions

1. Pretend the orange is a model of Earth.
   - What is the shape of Earth?
   - What does the orange peel represent in relation to Earth?
   - What does the white membrane represent in relation to Earth?

2. Why does the orange appear to be flat when cut into sections?

3. Why does Earth look flat rather than curved from where we live?

4. Name three different places where you might be able to see that Earth is not flat?

5. Why did people of long ago believe that Earth was flat?

Seismic Waves

Materials

- a globe or world map
- two wooden blocks
- a wooden table
- a Slinky®
- a Ping-Pong® ball
- a tub of water
- 10 feet (3 m) of rope
- a golf ball
- newspaper

Procedure

Open this activity by explaining that there are three types of seismic waves. Tell the class that you (along with some student volunteers) will be demonstrating how these waves travel through the interior of the earth and on the surface of the earth.

Primary/Pressure Waves (P-Waves)

Hand one end of a Slinky to a student to hold on to. Stretch the other end out and then let go of about 20 coils of the spring. Tell the students to watch carefully as the Slinky moves. It will move back and forth in a pushing-pulling motion. Explain that this kind of wave motion is like a primary seismic wave. It bounces back and forth, pushing and pulling as it penetrates through Earth's crust.

Secondary/Shear Waves (S-Waves)

Ask two students to each hold the end of a piece of rope. Have them move the rope from side to side to make a zigzag motion pattern. Explain that this kind of wave motion is like a secondary seismic wave that moves back and forth in a zigzag pattern. Secondary waves arrive after a primary seismic wave.

Surface Waves

Have a student demonstrate surface waves by pressing two wooden blocks together and sliding them up and down or from one side to another. Explain that the sliding motion of surface waves takes place on Earth's surface and causes the most damage during an earthquake.

Primary and Secondary Waves

Cover an area on the floor with newspaper. Fill a tub about ¾ full of water. Have a student hold a golf ball and a Ping-Pong ball about one foot above the tub and then drop the golf ball into the water. The ball will sink. Now have the student drop the Ping-Pong ball into the water. It will float. Explain that the golf ball penetrates through the water like a primary seismic wave. However, the Ping-Pong ball comes to a halt on top of the water just as a secondary seismic wave does not go further than Earth's crust.

Have a child drop a Ping-Pong ball and a golf ball onto a wooden desk and discuss the ways the two balls bounce. Explain that the golf ball acts like a primary seismic wave that penetrates deeply and loses a lot of energy through the wood. The students can touch the desk as the golf ball is bounced and feel it vibrate. When the Ping-Pong ball is bounced it acts like a secondary seismic wave that does not penetrate deeply.

Earthquake Engineers

Materials

- marshmallows
- short cocktail straws
- scissors
- hole punch
- two shallow boxes or cardboard trays (canned soda boxes work well)
- 10–20 marbles
- four rubber bands

Procedure

1. To make a shaker box, cut the bottom out of one of the boxes so that it fits down into the second box. Punch a hole in each corner of the cardboard piece. Feed a rubber band through a corner hole and hook it through itself to make a loop that is anchored in the hole. Repeat this process with the other three corners. Make a ¼-inch (.6 cm) cut in each of the four corners of the bottom box. Place the marbles into the bottom box. Float the piece of cardboard on top of the marbles. Loop the rubber bands through the short cuts in the corners so that the cardboard sits securely down over the marbles. The rubber bands should be taut but not too tight.

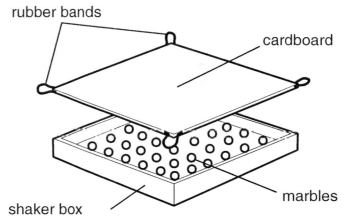

rubber bands

cardboard

marbles

shaker box

2. To construct the buildings, allow the students to make them alone or within groups, using straws and marshmallows. Each structure should be about 2 feet (61 cm) tall. To see how the structures hold up in an earthquake, place them in the center of the shaker box, pull the cardboard insert to one side, and let it go. This action will start the marbles rolling and simulate an earthquake. The students can experiment with the shaker box by pulling the rubber bands tighter, making them looser, or by shaking the bottom box.

Fundamental Facts

Earthquakes can cause tremendous damage to buildings and other structures. The collapse of buildings is the main cause of death and injury in earthquakes. Not only are people killed from being crushed, but they are also injured and killed by the falling debris of collapsing buildings. In earthquake zones, engineers and architects design buildings to withstand earthquakes. They design them so that they are flexible enough to rock and roll with the seismic waves. Before they begin to erect their buildings, they test models of them in a box called a shaker box.

Earthquake Safety

Emergency Earthquake Plan

Directions: Underline all of the things in each list that will help keep you safe in an earthquake. Discuss your answers with your friends or as a class.

1. **If I am at home during an earthquake, I will . . .**

    a. stand beside a window so that I can see what is happening outside.

    b. stay away from windows so that I do not get hit with broken glass.

    c. stay away from shelves so that falling objects will not hit me.

    d. get under a table, bed, or other heavy object and hang on until it's over.

2. **If I am at school during an earthquake, I will . . .**

    a. follow the directions given by adults.

    b. hurry to the office and call home.

    c. run as fast as I can to the playground.

    d. crouch down under a table or an inside wall, tuck my head down, and cover my neck with my hands.

3. **If I am in a store or business, I will . . .**

    a. get on the elevator so that I can get out of the building faster.

    b. crouch down on the floor near a wall or under a heavy table and cover my neck with my hands.

    c. get away from the windows.

    d. get out from between rows of shelves so that falling objects will not hit me.

4. **If I am in a car, I will . . .**

    a. get out of the car and hide under a bridge.

    b. stay in the car until the shaking stops.

    c. tell the driver to pull over to the side of the road.

    d. tell the driver to stay away from power lines, bridges, telephone poles, and trees.

5. **If I am outside, I will . . .**

    a. get to an open area where there are no trees, telephone poles, or power lines. I will then crouch down and cover my neck with my hands.

    b. run toward the closest house or building and start screaming.

    c. dive into the swimming pool, go under, and not come up until it is over.

    d. stay outside but get away from anything that might fall on me.

6. **After an earthquake is over, I will . . .**

    a. remind adults to turn off gas and electricity.

    b. use a fire extinguisher to put out small fires.

    c. go sightseeing so that I can look at all of the damage.

    d. only use the phone to report emergencies and injuries.

Volcano: The Eruption and Healing of Mount St. Helens

by Patricia Lauber

Summary

After remaining dormant for 123 years, Mount St. Helens, a part of the Cascade Mountain Range that runs down the western coast of the United States, erupted in May of 1980. It left behind 230 square miles (598 square km) of destruction on the north side of the mountain.

Patricia Lauber's *Volcano: The Eruption and Healing of Mount St. Helens*, describes the explosive eruption of Mount St. Helens and how life has slowly begun to return to normal in the area. Magnificent color photographs show each phase of the eruption, the destruction it caused, and the natural process of life returning to the mountain.

The outline below is a suggested plan for using the various activities that are presented in this unit. You should adapt these ideas to fit your classroom situation.

Note: Use Section by Section (pages 26–30) as a discussion guide for Lessons 1–5.

Sample Plan

Lesson 1

- Introduce the unit using the Volcano Bulletin Board (page 31) and Human Volcanoes activity (page 32).
- Read and discuss pages 1–8.
- Label the Parts of a Volcano diagram (page 33).

Lesson 2

- Read and discuss pages 9–26.
- Complete the Bulge, Blast, Surge activity (page 34).
- Experiment with gas bubbles (page 32).

Lesson 3

- Read and discuss pages 27–38.
- Begin the Splendid Spores activity (pages 43–45).
- Calculate the Volcano Facts (page 46).

Lesson 4

- Read and discuss pages 39–50.

- Continue the Splendid Spores activity (pages 43–45).
- Make a food chain and a web of life (pages 35–37).
- Do the Sprouts of Life activity (page 38).

Lesson 5

- Read and discuss pages 51–58.
- Illustrate The Ring of Fire (pages 62 and 63).
- Complete the Birth of an Island (page 61) and Coral Atoll Islands (page 39) activities.
- Discover Gushing Geysers (pages 50 and 51).
- Continue the Splendid Spores activity (pages 43–45).
- Begin the culminating activity, Volatile Volcanoes (pages 68–78).
- Assign other Across the Curriculum activities throughout this unit as you choose.

Overview of Activities

Setting the Stage

1. Make a large cross section of a volcano using the directions on page 31. Display it on a bulletin board for the remainder of the unit. Use it as an introduction to the unit and to show the parts of a volcano.

2. Do the Human Volcanoes activity on page 32 to give the students firsthand experience of how carbon dioxide gas warms inside their bodies, expands, and causes so much pressure that it "erupts" out of their lungs just as gas causes a volcano to erupt.

Enjoying the Book

1. It is recommended that this book be divided into short segments for better understanding of the concepts. The photographs in this book are outstanding. Attention and discussion should be given to each of them. A summary of the segments and discussion information is given in Section by Section on pages 26–30.

2. Use the bulletin board as an introduction to the Parts of a Volcano activity on page 33. Discuss the parts and inner workings of a volcano. Then ask the students to label their own copies of Parts of a Volcano. After checking their work, return the diagrams to the students so that they can use them for reference purposes throughout the unit.

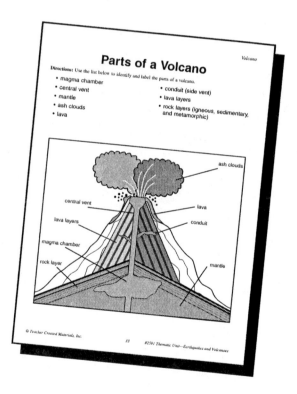

3. The activity Bulge, Blast, Surge on page 34 will challenge the students mathematically while teaching them more about the eruption of Mount St. Helens. They can also use the math problems to illustrate how the mountain looked before, during, and after the eruption.

4. Most children have experienced the surprise of a carbonated drink overflowing from its can. Use that experience to help them understand the intense force of gas under pressure. Instructions for this demonstration are entitled Gas Bubbles and are on page 32. (**Note:** This activity should be conducted outside.)

5. Help the students understand how fungi spores are spread and how they colonize other places. Use the Splendid Spores activities on pages 43–45. These activities will take more than one day to complete.

Overview of Activities *(cont.)*

Enjoying the Book *(cont.)*

6. Let the students further develop their knowledge of volcanoes by calculating the answers to the secret code in Volcano Facts (page 46).

7. To introduce the concept that all life is dependent on other life forms, have the students study The Food Chain and then build a Web of Life (pages 35–37). These activities will help them understand how they are also a part of the life cycle.

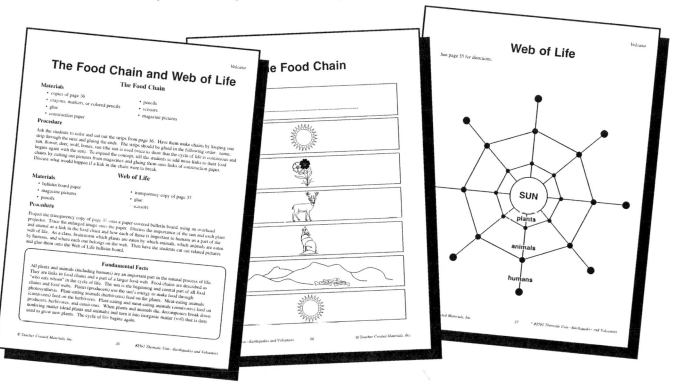

8. To extend The Food Chain and Web of Life activities, students can do the Sprouts of Life activity on page 38. During this activity they will see how seeds develop and mature into plants.

9. The students will better comprehend where most volcanoes are located and why they are located in these regions after completing The Ring of Fire exercises on pages 62 and 63.

10. Have the students read the short story on page 61, Birth of an Island, and then complete the activity at the bottom of the page. They will discover how volcanoes help to form some islands.

11. The students will learn how volcanoes help to create life in the ocean in the form of coral reefs by doing the Coral Atoll Islands activity on page 39.

Extending the Book

1. The students will learn about geysers by doing the math and science activities described in Gushing Geysers (pages 50 and 51).

2. Test the students on what they have learned about volcanoes by assigning the culminating activity, Volatile Volcanoes (pages 68–78).

Section by Section

Volcano: The Eruption and Healing of Mount St. Helens is filled with beautiful photographs and descriptive text that provide a vivid picture of life before and after an explosive volcanic eruption. It is recommended that short sections of the book be read to the students, discussed as a group, and then section-specific activities be done for reinforcement. The following can be used as a discussion guide so that the students can reap the greatest benefit from the book. Special attention can be directed toward the information that will be needed to complete the activities that follow each section.

Pages 1–8

What Is a Volcano?

A *volcano* is a geological land form, created from material that accumulates when hot liquid rock (*magma*) from the outer core forces its way upward through the mantle. The hot material either bursts out as cinder and ash or gushes out as a fiery hot liquid called *lava*. Layers of lava and ash form the familiar cone shape that most people associate with a volcano. Scientists can tell how many times a volcano has erupted by counting the lava layers.

The earth is divided into huge pieces called *plates* that float on the molten rock in the mantle. Most volcanoes are located along ridges where plates move apart or where two plates collide. Some volcanoes, such as those in Hawaii, form over *hot spots* where the tremendous heat in the mantle causes magma to rise toward the earth's surface.

Volcanoes are classified as active, dormant, or extinct. An *active* volcano is one that is erupting or may erupt at anytime. A volcano that is not erupting is called *dormant*. An *extinct* volcano is one that will probably never erupt again. There are about 600 active volcanoes on earth that produce at least 20–30 eruptions a year.

The appearance and name given to a volcano depends on how thick the lava is and how powerfully it is forced out of the vent.

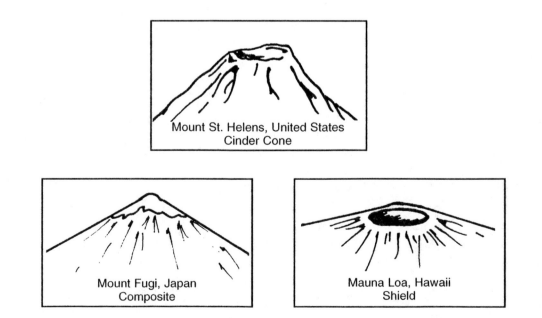

Mount St. Helens, United States
Cinder Cone

Mount Fugi, Japan
Composite

Mauna Loa, Hawaii
Shield

Section by Section *(cont.)*

━━━━━━━━━━━━━━━━━━ **Pages 1–8** *(cont.)* ━━━━━━━━━━━━━━━━━━

When magma contains a lot of gas, a huge explosion occurs as it is released. Melted rock, volcanic ash, rock, and mud pile up to form a *cinder cone volcano.* Cinder cone volcanoes look like flat-top mountains with steep sides and a wide, bowl-shaped opening. Thick, sticky lava flows slowly from this type volcano. Mount St. Helens is a cinder cone volcano.

Composite volcanoes are built from layers of thick lava, chunks of rock, mud, and ash. They are shaped like high-peaked mountains. Composite volcanoes have a single vent and alternative flows of slow, sticky lava and fast, liquid lava. Mount Fuji in Japan is an example of a composite volcano.

Shield volcanoes, like those of the Hawaiian Islands, are dome-shaped, low, and wide, with gently sloping sides that give a flat appearance. Magma can erupt from many vents at the same time. Fast-moving, liquid lava flows from shield volcanoes continuously over long periods of time.

Two Kinds of Lava

Pahoehoe (PAH-ho-eh-ho-eh) is the Hawaiian name given to quick-flowing, liquid lava. It forms smooth, ropy sheets as it cools and becomes solid.

Aa (ah-AH) is the Hawaiian name given to slow-flowing, sticky lava. When it hardens it has a rough surface. Both types of lava may flow from the same volcano.

Parts of an Erupting Volcano

Layers of *sedimentary, igneous,* and *metamorphic* rock make up Earth's crust. The crust is covered with soil and water.

The *magma chamber* is located about 3 miles (5 km) below Earth's surface. It contains hot, liquid rock called *magma,* trapped water vapor, and gases.

A vertical pipe called the *central vent* is formed as the magma mixture pushes toward the surface.

Conduits or *side vents,* that look somewhat like tree branches, may form along the sides of the central vent.

Lava is the name given to magma after it bursts through Earth's surface.

Overlays of lava, blistering-hot ash, pumice, steam, and mud explode out of the vents and clouds of ash blanket the area surrounding a volcano. Layers of this mixture combine to form the outside shape of the volcano.

Ash is the solid residue of combustion. The collection of tiny pieces of rock thrown from an erupting volcano is called *volcanic dust* or ash. The large pieces of rock are called *volcanic bombs.*

Section by Section *(cont.)*

════════════ **Pages 1–8** *(cont.)* ════════════

A *crater* is the opening or vent on top of a volcano. A *caldera*, or huge, circular crater, is formed when the cone of a volcano collapses into the magma chamber.

Volcanic Mountains

Mount St. Helens is part of the volcanic mountain range known as the Cascade Range. Most mountains are built very slowly through folding, doming, or faulting. Volcanic mountains are formed rapidly from lava flows containing rock, mud, ash, and dust. These mountains are more likely to be worn down quicker than others. When a volcanic mountain erupts, the pressure sometimes blows the whole top off. Mount St. Helens was 9,677 feet (2,951 m) high before it erupted explosively in 1980. After the eruption the mountain was 8,477 feet (2,585 m) tall—1,200 feet (366 m) lower.

════════════ **Pages 9–26** ════════════

Avalanches and Mud Flows

An *avalanche* is the sudden flow of a large mass of snow and other materials down a slope or cliff. Avalanches can reach speeds of over 100 miles (160 km) per hour. They can be triggered by temperature, moving snow masses, loud noises, and sudden vibrations such as an earthquake.

Mudflows after a volcanic eruption pose a serious hazard. The boiling heat from an eruption melts ice and snow on the mountaintop. The water mixes with ash and volcanic rock to form a thick mud-like mixture that moves rapidly down the mountainside. A mudflow at Columbia's Nevada del Ruiz volcano in 1985 claimed more than 25,000 lives.

Flash Point

Water turns to steam when it reaches 212° F (100° C) or boiling point. Before a volcano erupts, water stays liquid and is under tremendous pressure. It heats far above the boiling point and when it is suddenly released, the liquid explodes into steam. The pressure can be compared to that of a soda drink that has been shaken vigorously. When the cap is removed, the bubbles of gas in the drink suddenly escape, and the drink spurts out with great force along with the gas bubbles.

Volcanic Minerals

Pumice is a mineral formed when bubbles of gas are trapped in lava as it reaches the surface of the earth and cools immediately. Pumice contains many holes caused by expanding gas, making it light enough to float in water. Pumice is used as an abrasive in toothpaste, powder, and soap.

Section by Section *(cont.)*

━━━━━━━━━━━━━ **Pages 9–26** *(cont.)* ━━━━━━━━━━━━━

Seismometer

Geologists use *electromagnetic seismometers* to predict earthquakes. An electromagnetic seismometer records vibrations inside the earth that are analyzed by a computer. When magma moves inside Earth, it causes earthquakes that are recorded by the seismometer. The recordings help *volcanologists* (scientists who study volcanoes) predict when a volcano might erupt.

━━━━━━━━━━━━━ **Pages 27–38** ━━━━━━━━━━━━━

Survivors and Colonizers

Patricia Lauber compares the north side of Mount St. Helens to the surface of the moon, where no life exists. However, some forms of life can survive the tremendous heat and devastation caused by a volcanic eruption. The lush vegetation of the volcanic Hawaiian Islands are an example of how life can populate a bare, isolated land. Most of the plants considered to be native to the islands developed from seeds carried by ocean or air currents or by the droppings of migratory, fruit-eating birds.

Fungi and bacteria were two life forms found by scientists in the aftermath of the Mount St. Helens eruption. The fungi and bacteria worked together to decay and decompose the organic remains of plants, animals, and inorganic rock particles which, in turn, produced rich soil for plants to grow in. New plants developed in the fertile soil from seeds and spores that survived the eruption or were carried to Mount St. Helens by wind currents.

Plant seeds grow anywhere there is soil, water, and sun. Seeds are spread in several ways. Wind-borne seeds are carried to other places through the air. Prickly or sticky seeds are spread when they attach themselves to the fur coats of animals or clothing and are rubbed off in a different place. Some seeds are equipped with "wings" that allow them to float in the air for great distances. Other plants propel their seeds outward by popping them out of pods to scatter them in the wind. Water also helps to spread seeds by transporting them from one place to another with rain runoff or by washing them onto beaches close to the ocean.

━━━━━━━━━━━━━ **Pages 39–50** ━━━━━━━━━━━━━

Links and More Links

All life, plant or animal, depends on other life forms to survive. Pages 39–50 in the *Volcano* book describe how animals and plants form partnerships that help them survive. Many small life forms made it possible for plants and animals to return to Mount St. Helens to again support life.

Animals and plants must have food to exist. The sun is central to all life on earth. Life begins when organisms use the energy of the sun to make their food through *photosynthesis*. These organisms are the beginning of a sequence of life called the *food chain*.

Section by Section *(cont.)*

───────── **Pages 39–50** *(cont.)* ─────────

Food chains can be described simply by "who eats whom" in the cycle of life. Photosynthesizing organisms (plants) are called *producers* because they have the ability to produce food by using the sun's energy. *Consumers* are organisms that eat food made by the producers. *Herbivores* are consumers that feed directly on producers. *Carnivores* are consumers that feed only on consumers. *Omnivores* are consumers that feed on both producers and consumers.

Decomposers are organisms of decay, such as bacteria and fungi, that break down nonliving organic matter and turn it into inorganic matter to be used again by producers.

───────── **Pages 51–58** ─────────

The Volcanic Ring of Fire

Earth is divided into huge, moving pieces called plates. They float on the hot, liquid rock in Earth's mantle. Most volcanoes are located on ridges where plates move apart or where two plates collide causing one plate to go under the other. Hundreds of constantly active volcanoes are found in a belt located over the Ring of Fire. The *Ring of Fire* is a circular area around the Pacific Ocean along the continents of North and South America, Australia, Antarctica, and Asia. In this area plates are forced apart and collide with the continental plates, causing earthquakes and volcanoes. The Ring of Fire derives its name from the volcanoes that line its edges. Mount St. Helens is located on the Ring of Fire.

Volcanoes and Life

Volcanoes cause great devastation and destruction to life, but they are a part of Earth's natural processes. Forty-five million years ago Earth was a fiery hot planet where earthquakes caused volcanoes to constantly erupt. Molten lava poured out onto the surface and poisonous gases and water vapor were released into the atmosphere. Millions of years later Earth began to cool and the crust hardened. Violent storms raged. The water vapor condensed and became rain that formed the early oceans. Carbon dioxide reacted with the rocks of Earth's crust to form carbonate minerals that dissolved in the oceans. Primitive life, capable of photosynthesis, evolved in the oceans and began producing oxygen. Scientists believe that all of the oxygen in Earth's atmosphere was formed by a combination of carbon dioxide with water and photosynthesis and that volcanoes played a major part in the development of today's atmosphere.

Volcanoes still erupt today, and though they cause death and destruction, they also contribute to life on earth. Volcanic rocks are used for building materials and cleaning products. Useful chemicals are made from sulfur. Volcanic ash makes the land around a volcano very rich for growing crops. Valuable gemstones, such as diamonds, sapphires, opals, and topaz are buried in volcanic rock. Patricia Lauber states in her book, "The eruptions add gases to our atmosphere and water to our oceans."

Volcano Bulletin Board

Copy the volcano diagrams below onto transparencies. Project the transparency copy of diagram A (using an overhead projector) onto a paper-covered bulletin board. Use chalk, markers, or paint to transfer the projected image onto the paper. Now enlarge the transparency of diagram B onto a second piece of paper. Make sure the second image is enlarged to exactly the same size as the first. Trace diagram B. Cut out the paper copy of diagram B and attach the top of diagram B over the cross section (diagram A) on the bulletin board. Label the parts on the inside and outside of the volcano.

A.

B.

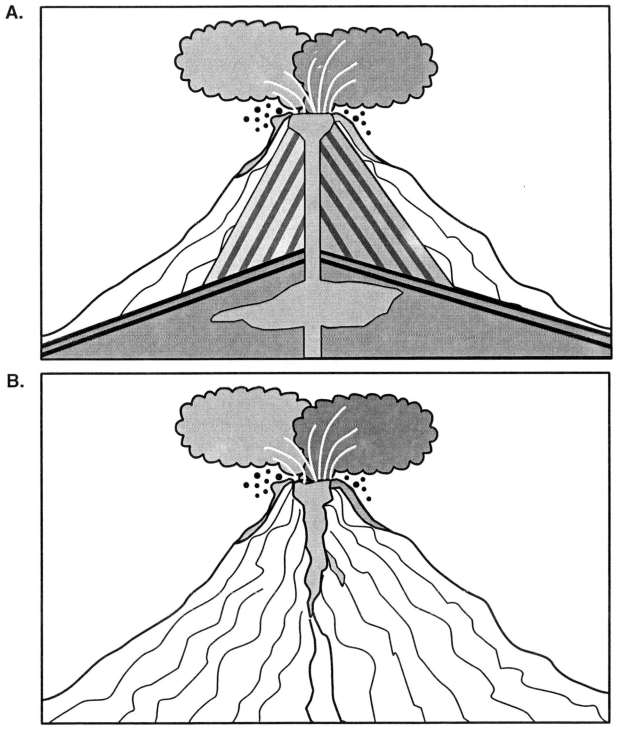

Pressure and Volcanoes

Compare the normal process of breathing to volcanoes by having the students do the two following easy experiments.

Human Volcanoes

- Ask the students to hold their hands about an inch (2.54 cm) in front of their mouths and feel the cool air as they inhale and warm air as they exhale.

Fundamental Facts

Explain to the students that when they inhale they take in a gas called oxygen that is used as fuel for their bodies. As their bodies use the oxygen, it turns into another gas called carbon dioxide. When the carbon dioxide gets warm, it expands and causes pressure to build up inside their lungs. When the pressure gets to a certain point, their bodies automatically push it out. This is a normal process that takes only a few seconds inside their bodies.

- Now ask students if they have ever taken a deep breath to see how long they could hold it. Discuss what they discovered. (It is impossible to hold your breath indefinitely, and when it is released, the air comes out with great force.)

Fundamental Facts

Explain that when a person holds his or her breath, carbon dioxide builds up in his or her lungs and forces an "eruption" so that the built-up hot gas can escape and new, cool oxygen gas can enter. A volcano erupts in much the same way. When hot melted rock, mixed with gas, pushes to the earth's surface, it blows out through a weak spot in the crust.

Gas Bubbles

- Demonstrate the intense force of gas pressure by vigorously shaking a carbonated drink and then opening it. Use a clear bottle so that the students can observe the build-up of small bubbles of gas. They will also be able to view the bubbles as the pressure is released when the bottle is opened. **Note:** Be prepared for the drink to spray all over. It is recommended that this experiment done outside.

Fundamental Facts

Explain that carbon dioxide gas is dissolved under pressure, which causes the emission of small bubbles of gas in carbonated beverages. When the pressure is released, the drink spews out along with the gas. The pressure of gas mixed with red-hot magma inside the earth is so strong that it pushes toward the surface, through solid rock, and is released as a volcanic eruption.

Parts of a Volcano

Directions: Use the list below to identify and label the parts of a volcano.

- magma chamber
- central vent
- mantle
- ash clouds
- lava

- conduit (side vent)
- lava layers
- rock layers (igneous, sedimentary, and metamorphic)

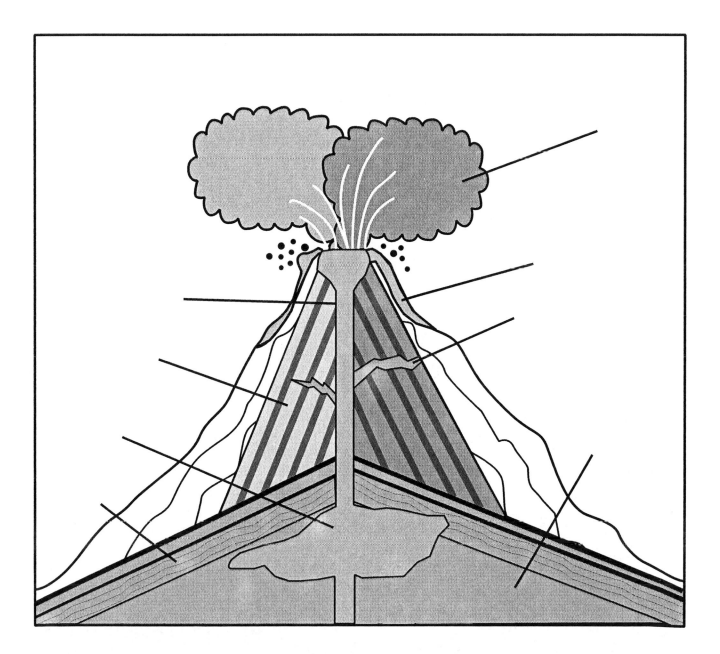

Bulge, Blast, Surge

Geologists make predictions about when volcanoes will erupt, based on the data they collect. Use the mathematical problems below to find out more about how they make their predictions.

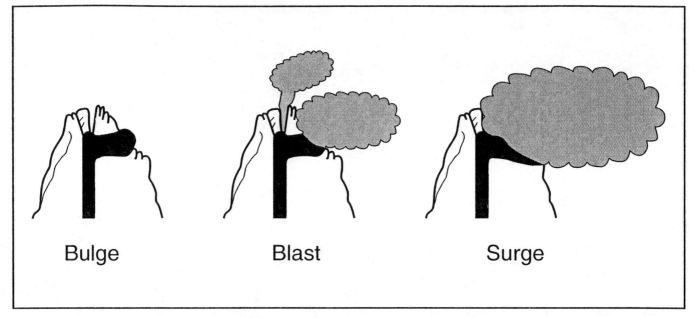

Bulge   Blast   Surge

1. Geologists measured the bulge on the north side of Mount St. Helens every day, beginning on March 27. The bulge grew 6 feet (2 feet) each day. Mount St. Helens erupted on May 18. How large was the bulge right before the eruption?

2. The bulge exploded at 8:32 A.M. In 4 minutes the ash cloud was 20 miles (32 km) wide. If the ash cloud grew at a steady rate, how wide was it at 8:33 A.M.? How wide was the cloud of ash at 8:37 A.M.?

3. Three feet (.9 m) of ash covered the mountain in 90 minutes. At this rate how much ash would have covered the mountain in one hour?

4. The eruption lasted for 9 hours and destroyed 225 square miles (585 square km) of trees. How many square miles of trees would have been destroyed if the eruption had lasted 12 hours at the same rate of destruction?

5. Mount St. Helens was 9,677 feet (2,991 m) high before the eruption. The explosion blew 1,200 feet (366 m) off the top of the mountain. How high was Mount St. Helens after the eruption?

Illustrate the following:

1. Draw a series of pictures that show what the bulge might have looked like before it exploded at 8:32 A.M., and how the ash cloud might have looked at 8:33 A.M., 8:34 A.M., 8:35 A.M., 8:36 A.M., and 8:37 A.M.

2. Draw a picture of the way the mountain might have looked after the eruption.

The Food Chain and Web of Life

The Food Chain

Materials

- copies of page 36
- crayons, markers, or colored pencils
- glue
- construction paper
- pencils
- scissors
- magazine pictures

Procedure

Ask the students to color and cut out the strips from page 36. Have them make chains by looping one strip through the next and gluing the ends. The strips should be glued in the following order: name, sun, flower, deer, wolf, bones, sun (the sun is used twice to show that the cycle of life is continuous and begins again with the sun). To expand the concept, tell the students to add more links to their food chains by cutting out pictures from magazines and gluing them onto links of construction paper. Discuss what would happen if a link in the chain were to break.

Web of Life

Materials

- bulletin board paper
- magazine pictures
- pencils
- transparency copy of page 37
- glue
- scissors

Procedure

Project the transparency copy of page 37 onto a paper-covered bulletin board, using an overhead projector. Trace the enlarged image onto the paper. Discuss the importance of the sun and each plant and animal as a link in the food chain and how each of these is important to humans as a part of the web of life. As a class, brainstorm which plants are eaten by which animals, which animals are eaten by humans, and where each one belongs on the web. Then have the students cut out related pictures and glue them onto the Web of Life bulletin board.

Fundamental Facts

All plants and animals (including humans) are an important part in the natural process of life. They are links in food chains and a part of a larger food web. Food chains are described as "who eats whom" in the cycle of life. The sun is the beginning and central part of all food chains and food webs. Plants (producers) use the sun's energy to make food through photosynthesis. Plant-eating animals (herbivores) feed on the plants. Meat-eating animals (carnivores) feed on the herbivores. Plant-eating and meat-eating animals (omnivores) feed on producers, herbivores, and carnivores. When plants and animals die, decomposers break down nonliving matter (dead plants and animals) and turn it into inorganic matter (soil) that is then used to grow new plants. The cycle of life begins again.

The Food Chain

See page 35 for directions.

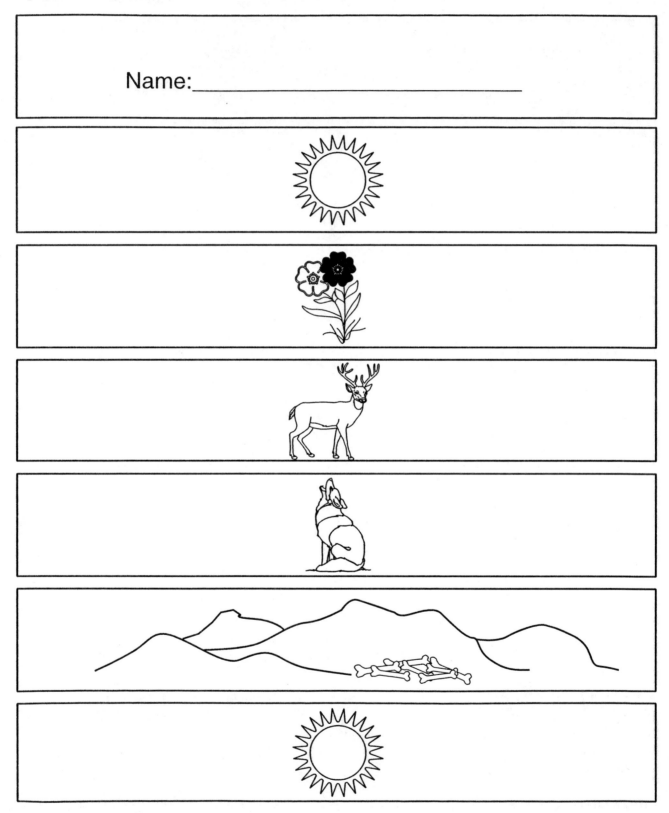

Name:_____

Web of Life

See page 35 for directions.

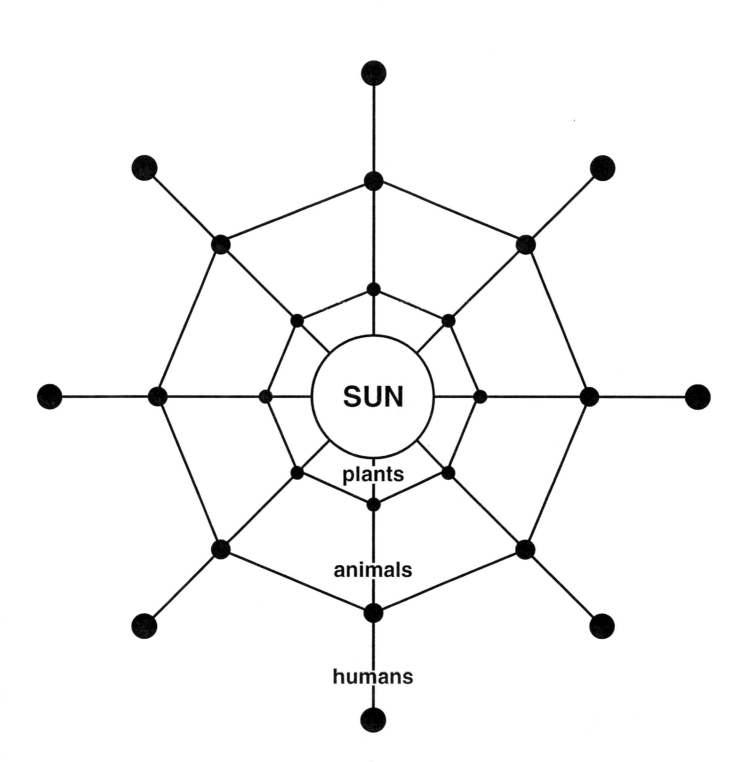

Sprouts of Life

Materials

- baby food jars with lids
- small nails
- alfalfa or rye grass seeds
- masking tape
- small hammer
- measuring spoon
- water
- permanent marker

Procedure

Before beginning this activity, use the hammer and nails to punch holes in the lids of the baby food jars. Wrap masking tape around each jar. Hand out the jars and have the students write their names on the tape labels using a permanent marker.

Tell the students to measure ¼ teaspoon (1.3 mL) of seeds and 4 tablespoons (60 mL) of water into their jars. Have them rinse the seeds and pour off any excess water. Next, tell them to put the lids back on their jars and set them in the sun. The seeds should sprout in a few days.

Note: Use this activity to stimulate a discussion with the students on the emergence of new growth after a volcanic eruption.

Hair Sprouts

Extend the above activity by using the sprouted seeds to make a "potato head."

Materials

- one large potato per student
- toothpicks
- craft glue
- red, glossy paint
- metal spoons
- potting soil
- plastic wiggle eyes
- paintbrushes
- paring knife
- shallow dish

Procedure

Let each student select a potato for this activity. Have them glue on plastic eyes and then paint on the rest of the facial features. Help the students cut off a slice of the potato at the top of each "head." Tell them to use their spoons to dig out a hole at least an inch (2.54 cm) deep. Have them put a small amount of potting soil into the hole, add their seeds from the above activity, and then put a little more potting soil on top of the seeds. Push three or four toothpicks into each potato to balance it so that it will stand upright. Place the potato in a shallow dish to avoid spillage. The students should add 1 teaspoon (5 mL) of water a day. The seeds will grow "hair" on the potato heads.

Coral Atoll Islands

Directions: Read about Coral Atoll Islands in Fundamental Facts below. Cut out the pictures and description boxes at the bottom of the page. On a separate sheet of paper, glue each picture next to the description that best matches it.

Fundamental Facts

Atoll islands are a group of coral islands, shaped in a ring or horseshoe, which grow over a sunken volcano. Atoll islands all have a large, shallow lagoon in their centers. The Marshall Islands, located in the central North Pacific Ocean, are a group of atoll islets and coral reefs. Kwajalein is the largest atoll in the Marshall islands. Many atoll islets and rings of coral are scattered throughout the channel that separates the Great Barrier Reef from the coast of Australia. The Great Barrier Reef, a chain of coral reefs off the northeastern coast of Australia, has the largest deposit of coral in the world.

How a Coral Atoll Island is Formed

1. An underwater volcano breaks through the ocean floor and erupts, sending red-hot lava high into the sky. The lava hardens as it hits the cool ocean water. The lava forms a small island that projects above the water.

2. After the eruption, the volcano begins to sink slowly back into the ocean. Coral builds and forms a ring around the sinking volcano.

3. The volcano sinks further into the ocean until it is no longer visible above the water. The coral continues to build around the volcano forming a shallow lagoon in the center of many coral islets.

4. Vegetation grows, and animals take up residence on the coral islets.

Seismic Story Starters

Reading, writing, listening, and speaking experiences blend easily with the teaching and reinforcement of science concepts. Science can be a focal point as you guide your students through poems and stories, stimulating writing assignments, and dramatic oral presentations. If carefully chosen, language arts material can serve as a springboard to a science lesson, the lesson itself, or an entertaining review.

One possible activity is to create stories about real or imagined events. A list of possible story starters is provided below.

1. All was still that night as I lay asleep. Suddenly, without warning, my bed began to gently rock back and forth as if it were on a rolling sea. I thought it was a dream. When I realized I was actually awake, I . . .

2. We were flying over beautiful, snow-topped Mount St. Helens. It was May 18, 1980. My family and I were on our way to Washington for a vacation. Suddenly, the top of the mountain exploded with such a force that rock and dust shot up into the air as high as our plane. Our pilot put the plane in a sharp turn to avoid this ominous cloud . . .

3. A vacation in Hawaii! My dream was about to come true. We packed plenty of swim gear and took the flight across the Pacific Ocean. It was night as we approached the islands. There was a strange red glow above the big island of Hawaii. I wondered aloud, "Could that glow be . . .

4. I am a scientist aboard a deep submersible vessel moving along the floor of the ocean. We are at a depth of about 4 miles (6.4 km), where sunlight cannot reach us. The only light is from the spotlight on our vessel. I look through a small porthole and I see . . .

Encourage the students to add illustrations to their stories. When they are finished, have them share their stories with the class. Have the students create covers for their stories and place them in the school library or arrange for the young authors to read their stories to students in other classrooms.

40

Earthquake Legends

Before the Activity

Tell the students to think about an earthquake experience they might have had and answer the following questions.

1. Where did it happen?

2. What time of day did it occur?

3. Where were you when it happened?

4. What did it feel like?

5. How did you feel during and after the earthquake?

After the students think of answers, let them share within small groups. Then select some students to tell the class about their experiences.

Explain to the students that although geology (the study of the earth) was developing in the 19th century, it was not until the late 1960s that scientists were able to explain the cause of earthquakes. Long ago, people who lived in areas where earthquakes occurred often made up stories to explain them. Tell the students that this lesson will introduce them to some earthquake legends. Then they will be able to write their own legend.

Materials

- white construction paper
- crayons or markers

Procedure

Read the legends on page 42 to the students. Encourage them to close their eyes and picture the stories as they are read aloud. Ask the students to locate the origins of the stories on a world map.

Have the students write their own fictitious stories about the causes of earthquakes. Ask them to also illustrate their stories. When they are done, let them share their stories and pictures in small groups. After the activity, display their creative works on a bulletin board.

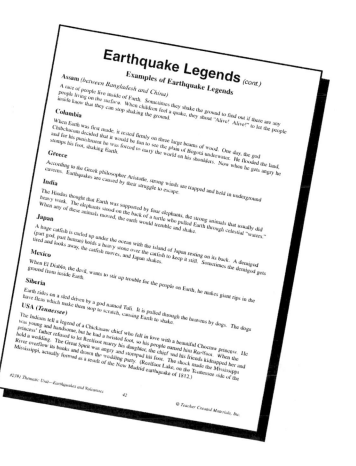

Earthquake Legends (cont.)

Examples of Earthquake Legends

Assam (between Bangladesh and China)

A race of people live inside of Earth. Sometimes they shake the ground to find out if there are any people living on the surface. When children feel a quake, they shout "Alive! Alive!" to let the people inside know that they can stop shaking the ground.

Columbia

When Earth was first made, it rested firmly on three large beams of wood. One day, the god Chibchacum decided that it would be fun to see the plain of Bogotá underwater. He flooded the land, and for his punishment he was forced to carry the world on his shoulders. Now when he gets angry he stomps his foot, shaking Earth.

Greece

According to the Greek philosopher Aristotle, strong winds are trapped and held in underground caverns. Earthquakes are caused by their struggle to escape.

India

The Hindus thought that Earth was supported by four elephants, the strong animals that usually did heavy work. The elephants stood on the back of a turtle who pulled Earth through celestial "waters." When any of these animals moved, the earth would tremble and shake.

Japan

A huge catfish is curled up under the ocean with the island of Japan resting on its back. A demigod (part god, part human) holds a heavy stone over the catfish to keep it still. Sometimes the demigod gets tired and looks away, the catfish moves, and Japan shakes.

Mexico

When El Diablo, the devil, wants to stir up trouble for the people on Earth, he makes giant rips in the ground from inside Earth.

Siberia

Earth rides on a sled driven by a god named Tuli. It is pulled through the heavens by dogs. The dogs have fleas which make them stop to scratch, causing Earth to shake.

USA (Tennessee)

The Indians tell a legend of a Chickasaw chief who fell in love with a beautiful Choctaw princess. He was young and handsome, but he had a twisted foot, so his people named him Reelfoot. When the princess' father refused to let Reelfoot marry his daughter, the chief and his friends kidnapped her and held a wedding. The Great Spirit was angry and stomped his foot. The shock made the Mississippi River overflow its banks and drown the wedding party. (Reelfoot Lake, on the Tennessee side of the Mississippi, actually formed as a result of the New Madrid earthquake of 1812.)

Splendid Spores

Materials

- copies of pages 44 and 45
- aluminum foil
- white bread
- quart-size (liter-size) resealable plastic bags labeled with students' names
- magnifying glasses
- scissors
- glue
- pencils
- water

Procedure

Prepare a bulletin board (away from bright light) to display the plastic bags. It should be located in a place that is easily accessible for student observations. If you do not have a board that is out of the direct light, staple a large piece of poster paper to the top of the board and let it hang loosely over the bags. The paper can be lifted for observations.

Find an open area outside, preferably out of the reach of animals, and roll out the foil. Give each student a slice of bread. Have the students place their bread slices on the foil and sprinkle them with a few drops of water. Leave the bread out overnight. The next day, have the students put each slice of bread in a plastic bag (be sure to label the bags with their names). Tightly seal the bags and staple them to the bulletin board. Make sure the students' names show. Provide magnifying glasses for observations and the journal records (page 45) for writing about their observations.

Ask the students to hypothesize about the following questions:

- Why was the bread dampened?
- Why was the bread left outside overnight?
- Why was the bread put into plastic bags?
- Why was the bread placed in a darkened area?
- What will happen to the bread?

Have the students complete the sequencing activity on page 44. Allow them to use magnifying glasses to observe the black mold growth. At the specific intervals suggested on the journal record (page 45), have them record their observations.

Fundamental Facts

Black bread mold has a fuzzy, spider-web appearance. It is a type of parasitic fungi that lives on non-living organic matter. It begins as a microscopic, airborne spore that germinates on contact with any moist surface of nonliving organic matter. It spreads quickly, forming a fine network of filament clusters that obtain food by absorbing it directly from the organic matter it has attached itself to. When the *sporangia* (knob-like spore cases) ripen, they break open, and the spores float in the wind until they land and begin the reproduction cycle again. Fungi and bacteria can be found anywhere other life exists. They work together to decay and decompose all organic matter.

Splendid Spores *(cont.)*

Materials

- white paper
- glue
- pencil
- crayons, markers, or colored pencils

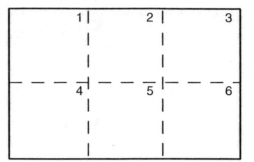

Procedure

1. Fold a sheet of white paper in half lengthwise. Fold the length into three equal parts. Crease the folds.

2. Open the paper. It should have six equal boxes. Number the boxes 1–6.

3. Put the title "Growing Mold from Spores" at the top of the page along with your name.

4. Cut out the sentence boxes below and arrange them in sequential order from 1–6.

5. Glue the sentences in order along the bottoms of the boxes.

6. Draw an illustration to represent each step.

Sprinkle a few drops of water on the bread.	Use a magnifying glass to observe the bread in the bag. Record changes on your Journal Record.
Put the bread in a plastic bag and seal it tightly.	Put a slice of white bread on a piece of aluminum foil.
Place the bag in a darkened area.	Put the bread outside and leave it out overnight.

Splendid Spores *(cont.)*

Journal Record

Directions: Describe the process that was used to collect spores on the bread slices. Keep a close watch on the bread slices and enter your observations below. Make entries only on the specific days listed.

Day 1—Describe the process for collecting spores on the bread slices.

_____

_____

Day 4—Observation #1 _____

_____

_____

Day 7—Observation #2 _____

_____

_____

Day 10—Observation #3 _____

_____

_____

Day 12—Observation #4 _____

_____

_____

Day 15—Observation #5 _____

_____

_____

Record any additional observations below and on the back of this paper.

_____

_____

Volcano Facts

Directions: Discover some interesting facts about volcanoes as you solve the problems. Use the code to solve the puzzle statements below.

A = 26 x 12 _____	J = 38 + 52 _____	S = 512 ÷ 16 _____
E = 16 x 11 _____	N = 77 + 19 _____	W = 1,173 ÷ 51 _____
I = 71 x 3 _____	R = 709 + 51 _____	D = 306 – 105 _____
M = 15 x 5 _____	V = 579 + 47 _____	H = 62 – 13 _____
Q = 39 x 4 _____	Z = 719 + 207 _____	L = 111 – 19 _____
U = 62 x 3 _____	C = 156 ÷ 13 _____	P = 999 – 555 _____
Y = 20 x 41 _____	G = 189 ÷ 9 _____	T = 818 – 319 _____
B = 627 + 11 _____	K = 104 ÷ 8 _____	X = 638 – 547 _____
F = 38 + 73 _____	O = 70 ÷ 5 _____	

1. A ___ ___ ___ ___ ___ ___ ___ is the huge, round crater which forms when the cone
       12 312 92 201 176 760 312
   of a live volcano collapses inward.

2. An instrument which can pinpoint the position of rising magma is called a
   ___ ___ ___ ___ ___ ___ ___ ___ ___ ___ .
   32 176 213 32 75 14 75 176 499 176 760

3. A special branch of geology that specializes in the study of volcanoes, especially those that are active or might become active, is called
   ___ ___ ___ ___ ___ ___ ___ ___ ___ ___ ___ .
   626 14 92 12 312 96 14 92 14 21 820

4. Volcanic ___ ___ ___ ___ ___ ___ ___ ___ ___ only began to be studied seriously in the
       176 760 186 444 499 213 14 96 32
   late nineteenth century.

5. Changes in a volcano are caused by ___ ___ ___ ___ ___ moving toward the surface to erupt.
       75 312 21 75 312

6. Volcanoes are also found on other ___ ___ ___ ___ ___ ___ ___ like Mars and Mercury.
       444 92 312 96 176 499 32

7. ___ ___ ___ ___ ___ ___ ___ ___ ___ eruptions of sticky, stiff lava commonly
   176 91 444 92 14 32 213 626 176

   produce one or more of these fragmental deposits: pyroclastic flows, ash falls, and volcanic mudflows.

8. ___ ___ ___ ___ ___ ___ ___ ___ ___ ___ ___ flows consist of glowing, hot
   444 820 760 14 12 92 312 32 499 213 12
   mixtures of pumice and ash.

9. ___ ___ ___ ___ ___ ___ ___ ___ are mixtures of fragmental, volcanic debris and water.
   75 186 201 111 92 14 23 32

10. A very light type of volcanic rock which can float in water is called
    ___ ___ ___ ___ ___ ___ .
    444 186 75 213 12 176

Predicting Earthquakes

Earthquake Probability

Materials

- copies of pages 48 and 49
- pencil
- map pencils or crayons
- calculator (optional)

Procedure

First, complete the math calculations below for the San Andreas Fault. Explain to students that the solutions (quotients) to these problems yield a percentage that indicates the probability of earthquakes in the places listed. Then write the percentages on the Probability Map (page 48). Finally, create a bar graph (page 49) that shows the areas along the San Andreas Fault in California where the probability of an earthquake is more likely.

Fundamental Facts

Seismologists predict a major earthquake will hit somewhere along the San Andreas Fault around the year 2000. Earthquake research shows that a major earthquake has occurred in California about every 150 years. Seismologist can predict the place and magnitude of a probable earthquake, but the time of occurrence can only be established within 30 years.

Percentage Math

Percentage calculations are used by scientists to evaluate data. After analyzing the data, it can be used to predict an earthquake.

Complete the following math calculations and convert them to percentages. Add the percentages to the cities on the Probability Map. Then complete the Probability Graph and questions.

1. 27 ÷ 45 = ._____ or _____% San Bernardino	**2.** 173 ÷ 346 = ._____ or _____% Eureka	**3.** 54 ÷ 90 = ._____ or _____% Los Angeles
4. 19 ÷ 21 = ._____ or _____% Parkfield	**5.** 116 ÷ 172 = ._____ or _____% San Francisco	**6.** Sacramento, the capital of California, is located in the same region as San Francisco. Create a percentage calculation that will equal 59% probability for Sacramento.

Predicting Earthquakes *(cont.)*

Probability Map

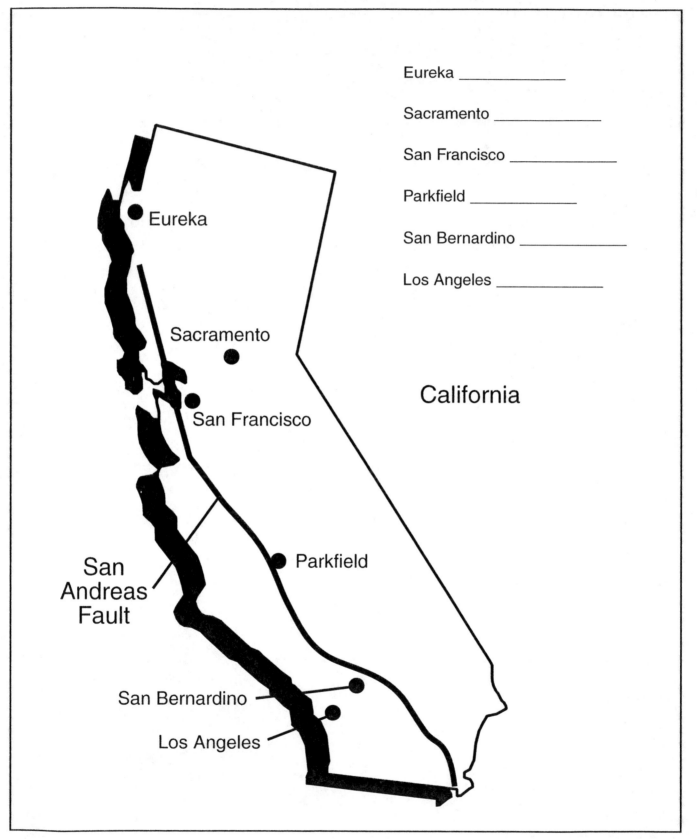

Eureka _____

Sacramento _____

San Francisco _____

Parkfield _____

San Bernardino _____

Los Angeles _____

California

Eureka

Sacramento

San Francisco

San
Andreas
Fault

Parkfield

San Bernardino

Los Angeles

Predicting Earthquakes *(cont.)*

Probability Graph

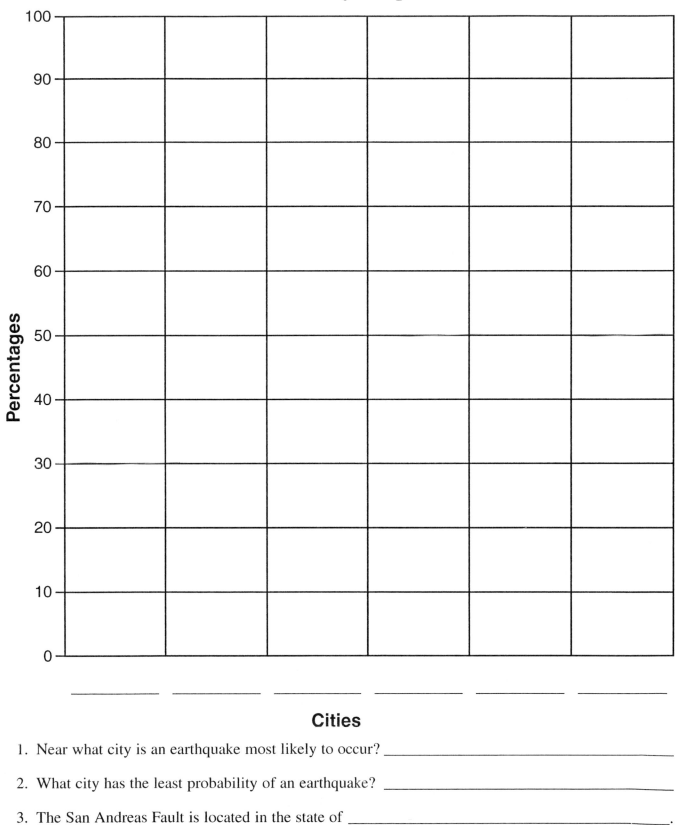

Cities

1. Near what city is an earthquake most likely to occur? _____

2. What city has the least probability of an earthquake? _____

3. The San Andreas Fault is located in the state of _____.

Gushing Geysers

Geysers erupt in much the same way as volcanoes, except geysers shoot out a fine misty spray of hot water. Groups of geysers can be found in New Zealand, Iceland, and at Yellowstone National Park in the United States. One of the most famous geysers is Old Faithful. It erupts about every 70 minutes. Old Faithful has erupted right on schedule for over 80 years.

A geyser develops over what is known as a "hot spot" where magma rises to within 2–3 miles (3–5 km) of Earth's surface and heats the rock layers all around it. Groundwater seeps into the heated ground and heats to a temperature above 500° F (260° C). As the water heats, it creates enormous pressure that causes the water to rise toward the surface. Sometimes the super-heated water reaches the surface to form a hot spring or a bubbling pool of hot mud. However, sometimes the water does not go all the way to the surface. It collects in an underground cavern or opening and begins to boil and produce pressurized steam. Finally, the pressure becomes too great, the steam pushes the water out, and the geyser erupts with a blasting roar. The water fills the cavern again and the process begins all over.

Old Faithful Math

Directions: Use the space provided to calculate the answers to the math problems below. Apply what you have learned about geysers.

---

1. If Old Faithful erupted at 1:55, at what time will it erupt again?

---

2. If Old Faithful erupts every 70 minutes, about how many times will it erupt in 24 hours?

---

3. If Old Faithful erupted 10 minutes ago at 9:17, how long will it take for it to erupt again? What time will it be when it erupts again?

---

4. Old Faithful usually continues to blast steam into the air for about five minutes. If it erupts about 20 times a day, how much time does Old Faithful spend blasting steam into the air in one day?

---

5. There are 365 days in a year and 24 hours in each day. How many times will Old Faithful erupt in a year?

Gushing Geysers *(cont.)*

Materials

- large glass container with flat bottom
- a straw
- a pin
- a nail
- small heat resisant glass bottle with a screw-on lid
- modeling clay
- food coloring
- hammer

Procedure

This activity is meant to be done as a demonstration for the class. Volunteers can help with some of the setup and cleanup.

1. Fill the small glass bottle half full with cold water. Add a few drops of food coloring to the water.

2. Carefully punch a hole in the screw cap with the hammer and nail. Make the hole large enough for the straw to fit through.

3. Push the straw through the screw cap.

4. Screw the cap onto the bottle and adjust the straw so that it is in the water but not touching the bottom of the bottle.

5. Seal the space between the straw and the cap with clay.

6. Wedge a small piece of clay into the top of the straw to seal it. Then use a pin to push a tiny opening through the clay.

7. Pour boiling water into the large container.

8. Stand the small glass bottle in the center of the bowl so that it is covered up to about the level of the cold water.

9. Watch as the air heats up and pushes the colored steam out of the tiny opening in the straw.

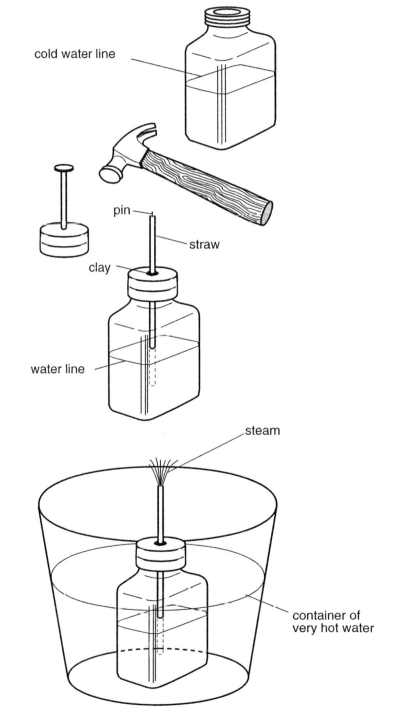

cold water line

pin — straw

clay

water line

steam

container of very hot water

Building Mountains

Fundamental Facts

There are four different types of mountain ranges: fold mountains, block mountains, dome mountains, and volcanic mountains. All mountains are formed as a result of movement in Earth's crust.

| Fold Mountains | Block Mountains | Dome Mountains | Volcanic Mountains |

Fold mountains are created when two tectonic plates collide and one plate goes under the other. All the land, rocks, and water between the two plates are pushed upward and crumbled into enormous folds. The Appalachians are fold mountains.

Block mountains are smaller than fold mountains. They are formed on fault lines when magma pushes up huge slabs of rock in the mantle, lifting up the land and splitting it apart. This creates wide rifts or cracks in Earth's crust. Great pieces of land slide down into the rifts, creating valleys with huge cliffs on both sides. The Sierra Nevada Mountains in California are block mountains.

Dome or *intrusion mountains* are created when swirling hot currents of magma push upward but cannot break through Earth's crust. The magma continues to press against the soil and rocks and finally spreads out in layers under the surface, forming a large rounded hump or dome-shaped mountain. The Black Hills of Dakota are examples of dome mountains.

Volcanic mountains are formed rapidly when gases in hot magma are forced upward through an opening or crack in Earth's crust. Lava slowly pours out the opening or erupts out violently forming a cone-shape mountain. The Cascade Mountains in the northwestern United States are volcanic mountains.

Building Mountains *(cont.)*

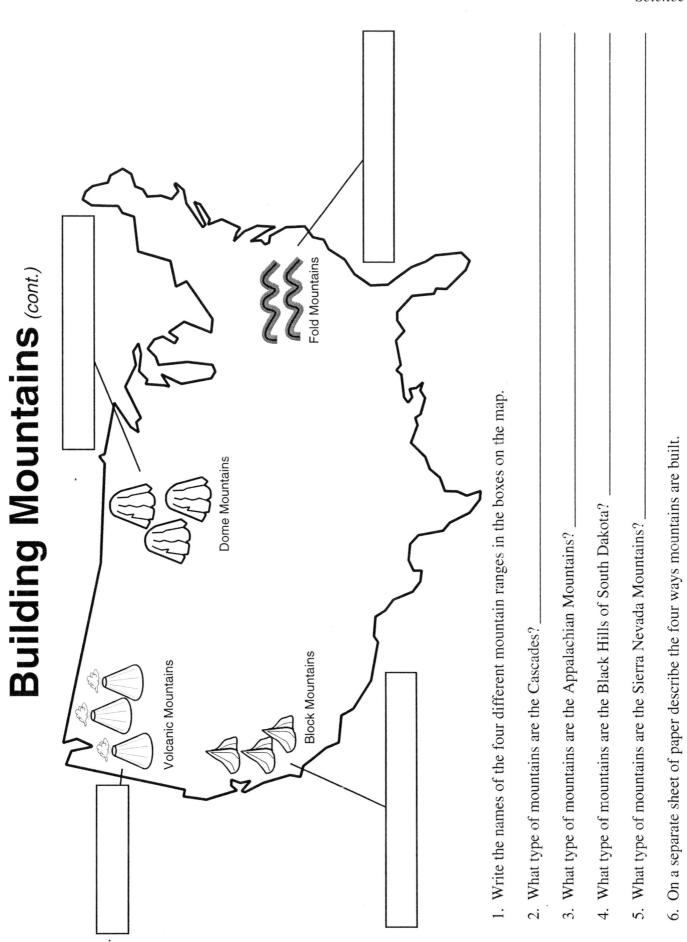

Fold Mountains

Dome Mountains

Volcanic Mountains

Block Mountains

1. Write the names of the four different mountain ranges in the boxes on the map.

2. What type of mountains are the Cascades? _____

3. What type of mountains are the Appalachian Mountains? _____

4. What type of mountains are the Black Hills of South Dakota? _____

5. What type of mountains are the Sierra Nevada Mountains? _____

6. On a separate sheet of paper describe the four ways mountains are built.

Folding Mountain Ranges

Materials

- graham crackers
- ice cream

Procedure

Layer ice cream between two graham crackers to make ice cream sandwiches for the students. Before they eat the sandwiches, have them squeeze the crackers together to see some of the ice cream ooze out. Tell them that in the same way ocean mud and land are squeezed when two plates collide.

Materials

- paper
- four different colors of modeling clay
- pastry roller
- tiny pieces of crushed rock
- green construction paper

Procedure

Before the students begin this activity, do a quick demonstration. Place a long piece of paper on a flat surface. Put one hand at each end of the paper. Push down as you slowly move your hands toward each other to create folds in the paper. Explain that your hands are like the giant tectonic plates floating on the mantle. As they move together, they crush and push everything in between upward.

Now give each student four small balls of modeling clay. Each of the four balls should be a different color. Have the students mix tiny pieces of crushed rock into one of the balls of clay. Tell them to roll each ball out into a 4"–6" (10 cm–15 cm) strip using a pastry roller. Tell them to stack the clay pieces on top of each other with the rocky clay as the top layer to represent Earth's crust. Then have them hold the layers on each end and push them together to form fold mountain models.

Divide the students into several groups. Have each group combine their fold mountains and arrange them on a piece of green construction paper to create a mountain range. Ask the groups to name their mountain ranges and display them for the rest of the class.

Fundamental Facts

The highest mountains in the world are fold mountains. Examples of fold mountains are the Alps in Europe, the Rocky Mountains and the Appalachians of North America, and the Himalayas in Asia. The world's highest mountains are the Asian Himalayas that were formed 40 million years ago. These mountains were built when the subcontinent of India and the continent of Asia collided and the northern edge of India crumpled and folded upward to form the Himalayas. The tallest mountain on Earth, Mount Everest, soars 29,028 feet or 5 $\frac{1}{2}$ miles (9 km) above sea level.

The Story of Rocks

The outer crust of Earth is made of a hard, solid material called *rock*. Earth's crust is about 30 miles (48 km) thick. *Geologists*, the scientists who study rock, classify it into three major groups.

Igneous rock tells the story of volcanoes. Igneous rock is formed when the hot liquid magma or lava from volcanoes cool and hardens. When magma cools below Earth's surface, it becomes *intrusive* igneous rock. When lava cools above Earth's surface, it becomes *extrusive* igneous rock. Obsidian and pumice are the two most common forms of igneous rock usually associated with volcanoes. Obsidian is a glass-like rock formed when lava flows out and hardens very quickly. Pumice is formed when gases bubble out of lava as it hardens, leaving holes in the lightweight, whitish rock.

Sedimentary rock tells the story of changes in the land and sea, of life long ago, and of climate changes. Sedimentary rock is formed from layers and layers of sediments such as sand, mud, shells, tiny pebbles, and decaying plants. These rocks are most commonly found on the bottom of lakes and seas where the weight of the sediment has pushed out the water from between the sediment and the material sticks together to form rock.

Metamorphic rocks tell the story of changes on Earth. Metamorphic means "changed in form." All metamorphic rock was once igneous or sedimentary rock that was changed by extreme heat or pressure. These are the hardest rocks on Earth and are used as a building material.

Minerals are the building blocks of rocks. There are over 2,000 minerals in Earth's crust making them the most common solid material on our planet. All rocks contain minerals and can be identified by the kinds of minerals that make up their composition. Talc is a very soft mineral used in talcum powder and chalk. The mineral pyrite looks like gold and is sometimes referred to as "fool's gold." Gold, silver, copper, aluminum, coal, and iron as well as topaz, rubies, and diamonds are all minerals found in rock.

The Rock Cycle

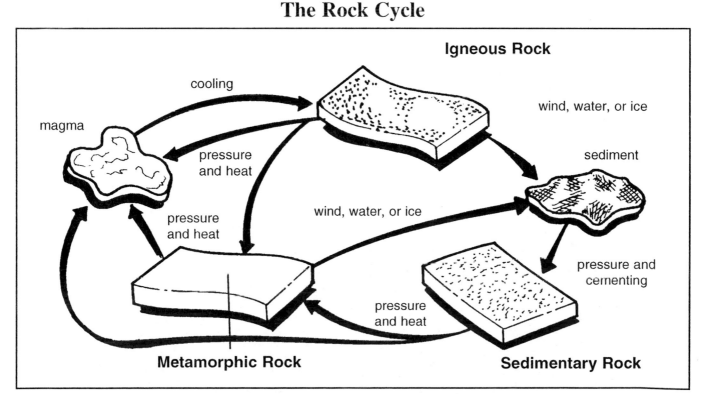

Rock and Mineral IQ

Identification Qualities

Materials

- copies of pages 57 and 58
- magnifying glasses
- eyedropper
- vinegar
- water
- pennies
- a glass jar
- a paring knife
- five sets of rock samples that should include: talc, pumice, pyrite, quartzite, limestone, obsidian, magnetite (These sets can be purchased at most teaching, science, or book stores at a reasonable price. Students should also be allowed to collect rocks from outside or bring them from home.)

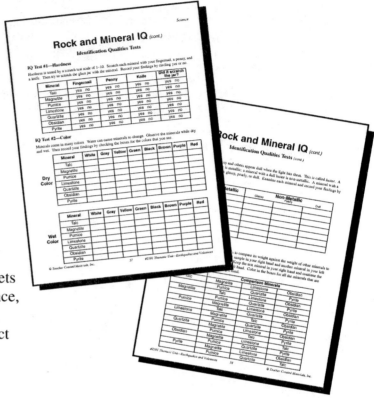

Procedure

After reading "The Story of Rocks" (page 55) with or to the students, help them to identify the rock and mineral samples. Tell the students that they are going to test the rocks' and minerals' identification qualities or IQ and that they will be able to observe that each has a special composition. Tell them that they will do the same kind of tests that geologists do to identify and classify rocks and minerals. Give the children copies of the charts. Have them conduct the tests as described on the charts. Set up testing centers at different locations in the classroom and allow the students to rotate through the tests. You may choose to divide the students into groups of two or three if there are a large number of students in the class. The students will perform the following tests: hardness, color, luster, weight and appearance. Discuss the results of their testing when they are finished.

Rock and Mineral IQ *(cont.)*

Identification Qualities Tests

IQ Test #1—Hardness

Hardness is tested by a scratch test scale of 1–10. Scratch each mineral with your fingernail, a penny, and a knife. Then try to scratch the glass jar with the mineral. Record your findings by circling yes or no.

Mineral	Fingernail	Penny	Knife	Did it scratch the jar?
Talc	yes no	yes no	yes no	yes no
Magnetite	yes no	yes no	yes no	yes no
Pumice	yes no	yes no	yes no	yes no
Limestone	yes no	yes no	yes no	yes no
Quartzite	yes no	yes no	yes no	yes no
Obsidian	yes no	yes no	yes no	yes no
Pyrite	yes no	yes no	yes no	yes no

IQ Test #2—Color

Minerals come in many colors. Water can cause minerals to change. Observe the minerals while dry and wet. Then record your findings by checking the boxes for the colors that you see.

Dry Color

Mineral	White	Gray	Yellow	Green	Black	Brown	Purple	Red
Talc								
Magnetite								
Pumice								
Limestone								
Quartzite								
Obsidian								
Pyrite								

Wet Color

Mineral	White	Gray	Yellow	Green	Black	Brown	Purple	Red
Talc								
Magnetite								
Pumice								
Limestone								
Quartzite								
Obsidian								
Pyrite								

Rock and Mineral IQ *(cont.)*

Identification Qualities Tests *(cont.)*

IQ Test #3—Luster

Some minerals appear shiny and others appear dull when the light hits them. This is called *luster*. A mineral with a shiny luster is metallic; a mineral with a dull luster is non-metallic. A mineral with a non-metallic luster can look glassy, pearly, or dull. Examine each mineral and record your findings by checking the boxes.

Mineral	Metallic	Non-Metallic		
		Glassy	Pearly	Dull
Talc				
Magnetite				
Pumice				
Limestone				
Quartzite				
Obsidian				
Pyrite				

IQ Test #4—Weight

One way to test the weight of a mineral is to compare its weight against the weight of other minerals to feel which one is heavier. Hold a mineral sample in your right hand and another mineral in your left hand. Ask yourself, "Which is heavier?" Keep the test mineral in your right hand and continue the weight test with different minerals in the left hand. Color in the boxes for all the minerals that are heavier than the test mineral in your right hand.

Test Mineral	Comparison Minerals		
Talc	Magnetite	Limestone	Obsidian
	Pumice	Quartzite	Pyrite
Magnetite	Talc	Limestone	Obsidian
	Pumice	Quartzite	Pyrite
Pumice	Magnetite	Limestone	Obsidian
	Talc	Quartzite	Pyrite
Limestone	Magnetite	Talc	Obsidian
	Pumice	Quartzite	Pyrite
Quartzite	Magnetite	Limestone	Obsidian
	Pumice	Talc	Pyrite
Obsidian	Magnetite	Limestone	Talc
	Pumice	Quartzite	Pyrite
Pyrite	Magnetite	Limestone	Obsidian
	Pumice	Quartzite	Talc

The Mystery of Atlantis

Atlantis has been described as "a mythical island continent that disappeared into the sea." Plato, a Greek philosopher, and the Greek poet Homer both wrote about the mysterious island. However, the two men disagreed about where Atlantis was located. Read the following stories about Atlantis and then complete a Venn diagram using the directions at the bottom of this page as a guide.

Plato's Atlantis

The Greek philosopher Plato described Atlantis as a paradise with a highly advanced civilization. According to Plato they had hot and cold running water and inside bath facilities with waste disposal systems. He told of fertile fields irrigated with water reservoirs and fruits, vegetables, and grains growing in abundance. The people of Atlantis were said to have worn gold, silver, and copper as clothing decorations, and they also used these precious metals to decorate their lavish homes. Plato believed the continent of Atlantis was located in the Atlantic Ocean between Africa and Europe. One day the island mysteriously disappeared into the sea. Accounts of the disappearance tell about earthquakes that shook the cities and of great walls of sea water drowning all of the people and sinking their beautiful island into the sea.

Homer's Atlantis

In the sea south of Greece lies an island that was very long ago inhabited by a group of people called Minoans. The Greek poet Homer described Atlantis as a great island, but most people considered his story fiction. In 1900 a curious archaeologist named Arthur Evans decided to find out the truth. He located the site where the city was supposed to have been and began to dig. Over the next 25 years, he unearthed and restored much of the fantastic city. The excavated ruins tell us of the Minoans' magnificent palaces and luxurious villas decorated with gold, silver, and precious gems. Their opulent homes had hot and cold running water, bathing and exercising areas, and elaborate drainage and sewer systems. They had many things in their homes that did not come from the island, and Evans concluded that they probably had a fleet of ships which sailed around the world trading for gold, ivory, and gems.

All the Minoan people suddenly disappeared. Stories tell of a violent earthquake followed by an explosive volcanic eruption that killed the people and covered their island with volcanic ash and mud.

Directions: Using the model at the right, draw a large Venn diagram on a separate piece of paper. Use the information above to complete the Venn diagram by writing statements from the stories in the correct sections of the intersecting circles.

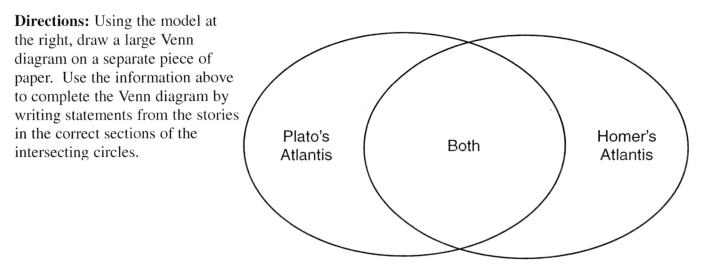

The Mystery of Atlantis *(cont.)*

Directions: Choose one of the stories about Atlantis on page 59. Retell the story by drawing pictures in the story frames below.

Birth of an Island

On a cold morning in November of 1963, a fishing vessel cruised off the coast of southern Iceland. At 7:30 A.M. the crew felt their boat sway irregularly and saw black smoke billowing upward in the distance. As their boat approached what they thought was a burning ship, the strong odor of sulfur filled the air.

Black smoke, ash, gas, and steam shot thousands of feet toward the sky. The crew of the fishing vessel was witnessing an awesome miracle of nature. A volcanic island was being born before their eyes.

Within a few days, the island of Surtsey, named after the Icelandic god of fire, was 200 feet (61 m) high and 2000 feet (610 m) long. In April of 1964, lava began to flow from the volcano, and as it cooled into hard rock, the island grew to 567 feet (173 m) above the water and more than a mile (1.6 km) long. Five years after the island of Surtesy had begun life so violently, green plants grew. Twenty-three bird species and 22 insect species had also made a home on the new island.

Islands in the Sea

Materials

- modeling clay
- plastic or foil tray approximately 12" x 18" x 5" (31 cm x 46 cm x 13 cm)
- water
- blue food coloring
- drawing paper
- pencils
- crayons
- water colors
- paintbrushes

Procedure

Divide the students into small groups. Have them mold mountain shapes out of clay. Tell them to attach the mountains to the inside bottoms of their trays. Next, have the students pour water in their trays, enough to it cover all but the tips of the tallest mountains. Color the water with blue food coloring.

Extension

After completing the islands in the sea models, extend this activity by having the students draw pictures of the mountains without water over them. Have them color their pictures heavily with crayons. Then allow them to use watercolors to paint the blue water over the pictures. Remind them that the tops of the undersea mountains should project above the water.

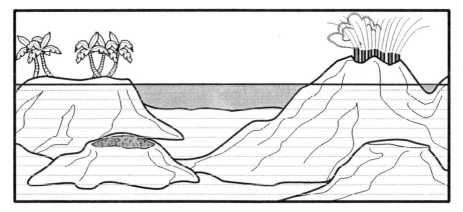

The Ring of Fire

Directions: Read the Fundamental Facts section and then carefully study the maps below. Draw the major tectonic plates on the world map on page 63. Draw volcanoes to illustrate the Pacific Ring of Fire.

Fundamental Facts

Swirling currents of heated particles, rising through the mantle from Earth's molten core, caused the outermost layer, the lithosphere, to crack like an eggshell. The cracked crust divided into seven large plates and 12 smaller plates. These plates float on the thick molten rock of the mantle. As the huge plates are pushed together, one will slip along the edges of the other, slide down under the other, or thrust up over the other. Any of these actions—slip, slide, or thrust—may take place at convergent and subduction zones where 70 percent of all volcanic eruptions and earthquakes occur. Along mid-ocean rifts or ridges, plates mainly separate and red-hot magma pours out, adding new crust material to the ocean floor.

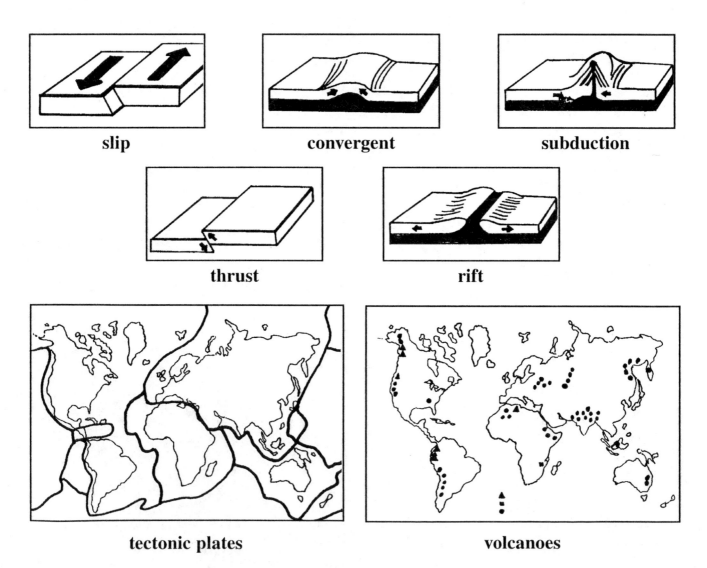

slip   **convergent**   **subduction**

thrust   **rift**

tectonic plates   **volcanoes**

The Ring of Fire (cont.)

World Map

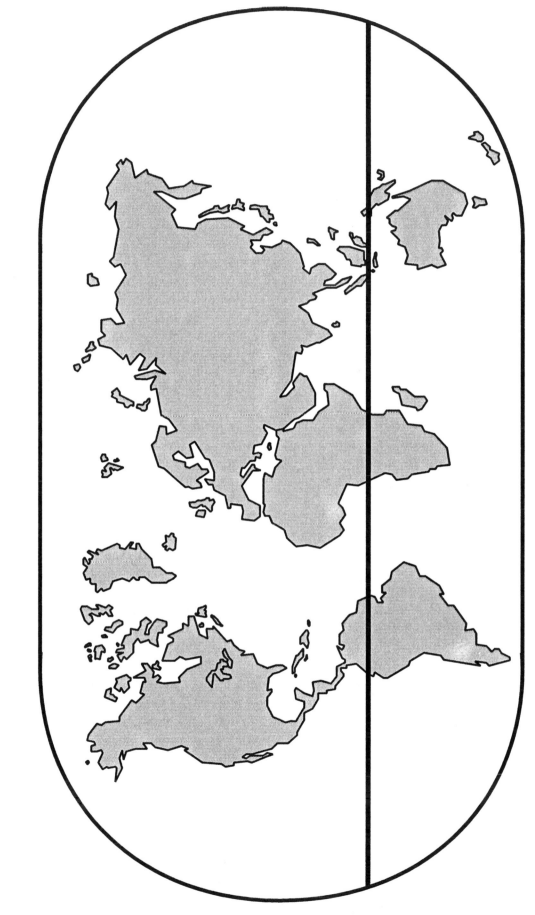

Salt Sculptures

Materials

- salt dough (recipe below)
- blue and green food coloring
- three pieces of white poster board
- sharp knife
- paper
- pencil
- white glue
- transparency copy of the three pictures on page 65

Salt Dough Recipe

Combine 4 cups (960 mL) flour, 1 cup (240 mL) salt, 1 ½ cups (360 mL) water, 2 tablespoons (30 mL) baby oil, 2 teaspoons (10 mL) alum (which can be purchased at most pharmaceutical counters). Knead dough until mixed well. No cooking is necessary.

Procedure

Make three batches of salt dough. Divide each batch into four equal balls. Use food coloring to dye three balls blue and one ball green. Make a transparency copy of the three pictures on page 65. Project the pictures onto a screen or wall where everyone can see them. Explain to the students that the three blue balls represent water and the green ball represents land. Tell them that water covers ³/₄ of Earth while land covers only ¼. Divide the students into three groups. Assign each group one of the pictures on page 65 to reproduce, using the salt dough and the directions below. (**Note:** If possible, enlarge the pictures to at least 24" or 61 cm in diameter.) After the assignment is complete, have each group explain their sculptures to the others in the class and then have each student write a short essay describing his or her sculpture.

Directions for Making Salt Sculptures

1. Cut around the outside of the land forms in the picture, leaving all of the connections intact.

2. Lay the ball of green dough in the center of your piece of poster board. Flatten the green dough until it is large enough that the cutout land forms will fit over it.

3. Lay the paper land forms over the green dough. Use the knife (or have your teacher use the knife) to carefully cut around the land forms in the picture. Use a pencil to trace the lines on any land forms that are still connected, being careful not to cut through the dough. Remove the paper and the excess green dough. Glue down the outside edges of the green dough to hold it in place.

4. Flatten the blue dough and form a circular shape around the outside of the green dough. Also, use the blue dough to fill in where water separates the land forms.

5. Glue down the blue dough to secure it in place.

6. Allow the dough sculpture to dry overnight. Add a title and the names of the participating students.

Salt Sculptures *(cont.)*

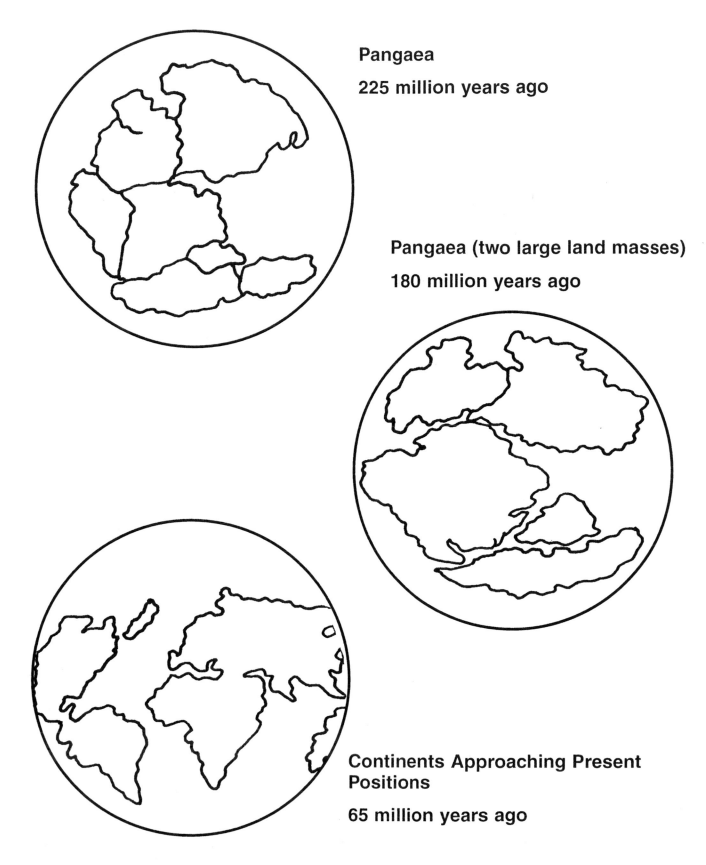

Pangaea

225 million years ago

Pangaea (two large land masses)

180 million years ago

Continents Approaching Present
Positions

65 million years ago

Model of Earth

Inner and Outer Layers

Materials

- scissors
- one copy of page 67 per student
- 8 ½" x 11" (22 cm x 28 cm) brown, orange, yellow, and red construction or index paper
- stapler
- pencil or markers
- compass for drawing circles

Directions

1. Distribute a copy of page 67 to each student. Explain that students will make a model demonstrating the location of Earth's crust, mantle, outer core, and inner core.

2. Draw a diagram of the four layers and label each layer as shown on the right. Provide students with a variety of resources and discuss with them basic facts about each layer.

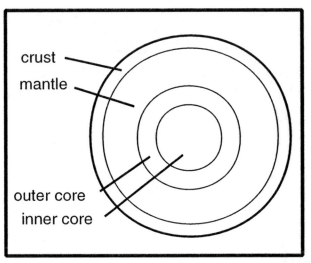

3. Provide each student with a piece of brown, orange, yellow, and red construction or index paper. Have students use a compass to draw a 6" (15 cm) circle on each piece of paper. Cut out the circles.

4. Have students cut out diamond shapes in the center of each circle. Use the measurements provided in the diagrams on page 67 as a guide. Students should label the layers according to the diagrams.

5. Assemble the circles in the following order, from top to bottom: cover (picture of Earth), brown circle, orange circle, yellow circle, and red circle.

6. Ask students to add some facts about each layer on the correct circles.

7. Lift the top circle to reveal all of the interior layers through the diamond-shaped windows. Then, lift each layer separately to see its name and read the related information.

Model of Earth *(cont.)*

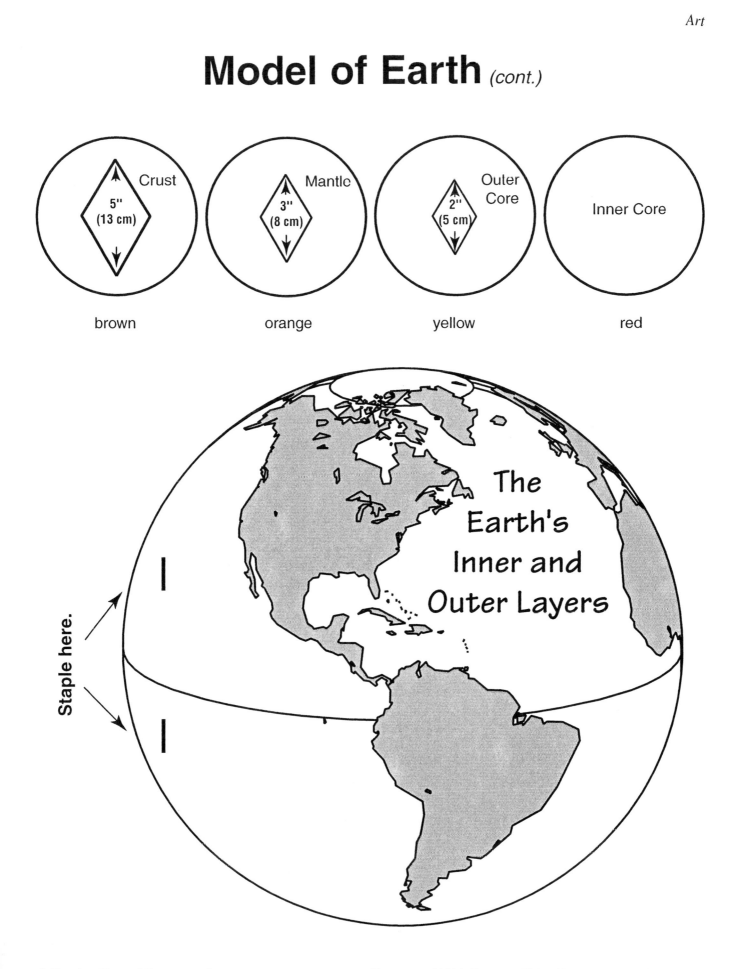

Crust
5"
(13 cm)

brown

Mantle
3"
(8 cm)

orange

Outer
Core
2"
(5 cm)

yellow

Inner Core

red

Staple here.

The Earth's Inner and Outer Layers

Volatile Volcanoes

Performance-Based Assessments

In recent years many school districts have been moving toward Performance-Based Assessments that include several given tasks in a certain area of the curriculum, a rubric scoring guide for each task, and a self-scoring guide for the students. Writing is an important part of these assessments.

The following Performance-Based Assessments for volcanoes can be used as a guide to assess the students' knowledge based on a rubric-scoring scale of advanced, proficient, basic, and below basic. To be considered "at grade level," the students must reach the proficient level on all given tasks in an assessment.

Four student-learning tasks of increasing difficulty are included as a part of the volcano assessment. Also included are the Teacher Scoring Guide for each task and a generic Student Scoring Guide that can be used for all of the tasks.

If you would like to assess your students' learning from the Earthquakes section of this unit, use these volcano tasks as a model to create your own Performance-Based Assessment.

Complete teacher instructions, a materials list, procedures, and "Fundamental Facts" for making volcanoes are given on page 69.

Outline of Student-Learning Tasks

Task 1: Volatile Volcanoes

The students will construct a model of a volcano. They will use a chemical mixture to create a volcanic eruption.

Task 2: Descriptive Writing

The students will create a descriptive writing selection that will include a step-by-step description of how they built the volcano and an explanation of the chemical process that made it erupt.

Task 3: Compare and Contrast

The students will use a Venn diagram to compare their model volcano to a real volcano. They will also explain in writing how their model is alike and different from a real volcano.

Task 4: Volcano Research

The students will use the information in this unit, computers, the library, and other information sources to research volcanoes. They will each choose a specific volcano (for example, Mount St. Helens) as the subject of a written research report that will include the kind of volcano, location, data on its most recent eruption, description of the eruption, probable cause of the eruption, and destruction caused by the eruption.

Volatile Volcanoes *(cont.)*

Teacher Directions for Student Task 1

Materials

- white glue
- 2 gal (8 L) of vinegar
- liquid dish soap

- one pound (.45 kg) of baking soda
- red food coloring
- permanent marker

Materials Per Student

- baby food jar or small glass
- 8-ounce (240 mL) paper cup
- plastic spoon

- large Styrofoam plate
- 4-ounce (120 mL) paper cup
- two sticks of modeling clay or one can of prepared colored dough

Procedure

Tell the students to label the edges of their plates with their names in permanent marker. Have them each place a baby food jar in the middle of their plates. Next, tell them to roll their clay to make two snake-shaped pieces each. Beginning at the bottom, have them wrap their clay around their jars and then press it to flatten it against the jars. They can then use their second piece of clay to wrap around the first layer to create the shape of a cone volcano. This layer should also be smoothed with their fingers.

Using paintbrushes, the students can apply white glue all over their volcanoes. After the glue has dried, they should apply a second coat to make sure that all of the clay surfaces are covered with a thick layer of glue as a seal. Tell them to wipe out the insides of the jars with clean wet cloths after each glue application. Let the volcanoes dry until the glue is hard, usually overnight.

Erupting Volcanoes

Fill the students' 8-ounce cups with vinegar. Have students add a drop of red food coloring and a drop of liquid dish soap to each cup. Fill their 4-ounce cups with baking soda.

Give each student the volcano that they made earlier, an 8-ounce cup of vinegar, a 4-ounce cup of baking soda, and a plastic spoon.

Have them put a teaspoonful of baking soda into their volcanoes and then pour the vinegar slowly over the baking soda, just until the liquid begins to bubble over the top. Tell them to stop pouring and watch their volcanoes erupt. Pour the excess liquid off the plates after each eruption. (**Note:** Pouring it in a sink will actually help clean the pipes and keep them flowing.)

Fundamental Facts

When baking soda and vinegar are mixed they create a new substance. The atoms and molecules are rearranged to produce a gas called carbon dioxide. When you create a new substance by mixing things together, you have caused a chemical reaction to occur.

Volatile Volcanoes *(cont.)*

Student Task 1

Follow the directions below to make a model of a volcano. Show your teacher and the other students as your volcano erupts. Score your work, using the Student Scoring Guide on page 74.

Materials Needed to Make a Volcano

- a baby food jar
- a permanent marker
- white glue
- a damp cloth
- a Styrofoam plate
- two sticks of modeling clay
- a paintbrush

Directions

1. Put your name on the edge of the plate with a permanent marker.
2. Place a baby food jar in the center of the plate.
3. Take some clay and roll it to make two "snake" shapes.
4. Beginning at the bottom of the jar, wrap a piece of clay around the jar and press it to flatten it against the jar. Shape the second piece of clay around the outside of the jar and smooth it with your fingers to resemble the shape of a volcano.
5. Using the paintbrush, apply white glue all over the volcano.
6. Let your volcano dry and apply a second coat of glue to make sure that all of the clay surfaces are covered with a thick layer of glue.
7. Wipe out the inside of the jar with a clean damp cloth after each glue application.
8. Let the volcano dry until the glue is hard, usually overnight.

Materials Needed to Make the Volcano Erupt

- a plastic spoon
- a large paper cup filled with vinegar
- a drop of liquid soap
- a small paper cup filled with baking soda
- a drop of red food coloring

Directions

1. Read all of the directions before you begin.
2. Put a teaspoonful of baking soda in your volcano.
3. Pour the vinegar mixture slowly over the baking soda, just until the liquid begins to bubble over the top. Stop pouring and watch the volcano erupt. Pour the excess liquid off the plate and into a sink each time you erupt your volcano.
4. Discuss as a class how baking soda and vinegar form a chemical reaction to make your model volcano look like it is erupting.

Volatile Volcanoes *(cont.)*

Student Task 2

Write a step-by-step description of how you made your volcano and what your volcano looks like. Also explain how you made your volcano erupt. If you need more writing space, continue your work on a separate piece of paper. Add a title to your work. Draw a picture of your volcano on a piece of white paper. Score your work using the Student Scoring Guide on page 74.

_____

(Title)

_____

_____

_____

_____

_____

_____

_____

_____

_____

_____

_____

_____

_____

_____

_____

_____

Volatile Volcanoes *(cont.)*

Student Task 3

Read the following information about volcanoes. Use the Venn diagram at the bottom of the page to compare your volcano model with a real volcano. On a separate sheet of paper write a paragraph that gives at least two ways your model is alike and two ways it is different from a real volcano. Score your work using the Student Scoring Guide on page 74.

Volcanoes

Below Earth's thin outer crust, just 20–25 miles (32–40 km) below your feet, is a thick layer of rock called the *mantle*. The temperature in the mantle is so hot that the rock has melted and turned into a thick, fiery liquid called *magma*. The magma shifts and churns, causing gas bubbles to form. Pressure builds and pushes the magma upward toward Earth's surface, through a central vent in places where the crust is cracked or weak. With a deafening explosion, hot gases, steam, dust, and pieces of rock burst through the surface. The explosion is followed by rivers of fiery, red magma which is called *lava* when it reaches the surface. Sometimes lava gushes out of a volcano quietly, spilling over the top and down the sides at speeds of over 40 miles (64 km) per hour. Layers of lava and ash form the familiar cone shape that most people associate with a volcano. Scientists can tell how many times a volcano has erupted by counting the lava layers. A volcano is a geological land form, created from material that accumulates when a volcano erupts.

Volcano Venn Diagram

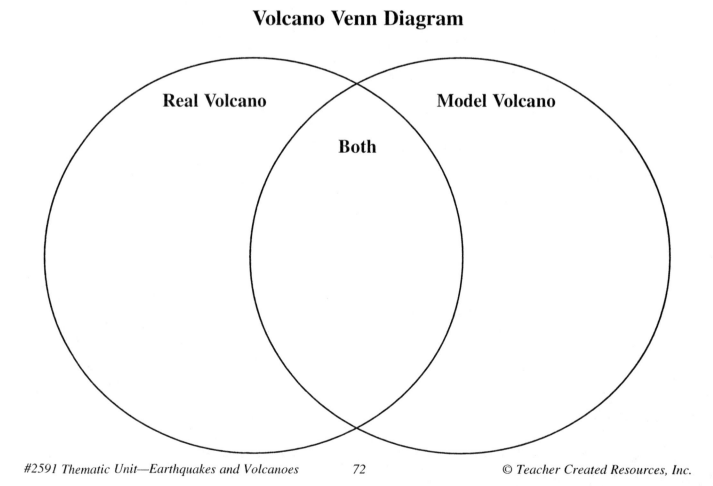

Volatile Volcanoes *(cont.)*

Student Task 4

Use a computer and the Internet, the school library, and other resources to research volcanoes. Select a specific volcano and write a research report about it. In your report include the kind of volcano it is, where it is located, when it last erupted, a description of the eruption, and a description of the destruction the eruption caused. Be sure to list the sources that you used in your report. A list of vocabulary words that you might use in your report is given below. Score your work, using the Student Scoring Guide on page 74.

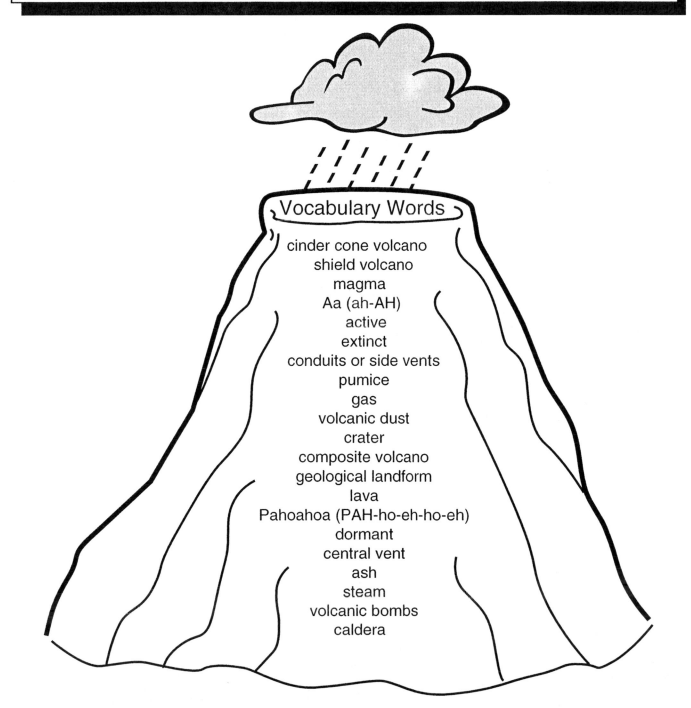

Vocabulary Words

cinder cone volcano
shield volcano
magma
Aa (ah-AH)
active
extinct
conduits or side vents
pumice
gas
volcanic dust
crater
composite volcano
geological landform
lava
Pahoahoa (PAH-ho-eh-ho-eh)
dormant
central vent
ash
steam
volcanic bombs
caldera

Volatile Volcanoes *(cont.)*

Student Scoring Guide

Directions: Read the three sections below. Choose the section you feel best describes you. Place a check mark in the boxes (in that section) next to the statements with which you agree. Complete the statements with blank lines.

★ ★ ★

☐ I read and followed the directions.

☐ I completed the task by exactly following the directions.

☐ I think I did an especially good job because_____

_____

_____ .

★ ★

☐ I needed help to read and follow the directions.

☐ I completed the task with help from my teacher and others.

☐ I will keep trying because I can almost do it alone.

☐ I think I did my best work on_____

_____

_____ .

★

☐ I could not read and understand the directions.

☐ I did not complete the task.

☐ I will work hard and keep trying.

Volatile Volcanoes *(cont.)*

Teacher Scoring Guide for Student Task 1

Directions: Put check marks in all of the boxes that apply in a specific category. A place for writing notes is given following each category.

4—Advanced

☐ The student read the directions without help from the teacher.

☐ The student assembled the materials needed and constructed the volcano model without help from the teacher.

☐ The student could cause his or her model to erupt for the teacher and other students.

☐ The student could explain orally to the teacher and other students how he or she made the volcano. The directions the student gave were clear and in sequential order.

☐ The student could explain to the teacher and other students the chemicals used to make the volcano model erupt.

Notes:_____

3—Proficient

☐ The student read the directions without help from the teacher.

☐ The student assembled the materials needed and constructed the volcano model without help from the teacher.

☐ The student could cause his or her model to erupt for the teacher and other students.

Notes:_____

2—Basic

☐ The student needed the teacher's help to read and follow the directions.

☐ The student completed the volcano model with help from the teacher and other students.

☐ The student could make the volcano model erupt.

☐ The student should repeat this task until he or she is proficient.

Notes:_____

1—Below Basic

☐ The student could not read or understand the directions.

☐ The student needed a lot of assistance in making and erupting the model volcano.

☐ The student needed teacher assistance to erupt the volcano model.

☐ The student did not complete the project.

☐ The student should repeat the task until he or she is proficient.

Notes:_____

Volatile Volcanoes *(cont.)*

Teacher Scoring Guide Student Task 2

Directions: Put check marks in all of the boxes that apply in a specific category. A place for writing notes is given following each category.

4—Advanced

☐ The student wrote a step-by-step description of how he or she made the volcano model and a description of what the model looked like.

☐ The student explained how he or she made the volcano model erupt.

☐ The student put a title on his or her work.

☐ The student drew an illustration of his or her volcano model.

☐ The student spelled words correctly and used correct punctuation.

☐ The student included words learned in the volcano unit in his or her description. (Some vocabulary words are listed in Task 4 on page 73.)

Notes:_____

3—Proficient

☐ The student wrote a step-by-step description of how he or she made the volcano model and a description of what the model looked like.

☐ The student explained how he or she made the volcano erupt.

☐ The student put a title on his or her work.

☐ The student drew an illustration of his or her volcano model.

☐ The student spelled words correctly and used correct punctuation.

Notes:_____

2—Basic

☐ The student needed help with the entire writing assignment.

☐ The student tried to draw an illustration of his or her volcano model.

☐ The student spelled some words incorrectly and did not always use correct punctuation.

☐ The student should repeat this task until he or she is proficient.

Notes:_____

1—Below Basic

☐ The student did not complete the writing task.

☐ The student should repeat this task until he or she is proficient.

Notes:_____

Volatile Volcanoes *(cont.)*

Teacher Scoring Guide for Student Task 3

Directions: Put check marks in all of the boxes that apply in a specific category. A place for writing notes is given following each category.

4—Advanced

☐ The student read the information without teacher assistance.

☐ The student compared the model volcano to a real volcano, using the Venn diagram.

☐ The student wrote a paragraph that stated two ways the model and the real volcano are alike and two ways they are different.

☐ The student used correct spelling and punctuation.

☐ The student gave more than two examples of how the model and a real volcano are alike and different.

Notes:_____

3—Proficient

☐ The student read the information without teacher assistance.

☐ The student compared the model volcano to a real volcano, using the Venn diagram.

☐ The student wrote a paragraph that stated two ways the model and the real volcano were alike and two ways they are different.

☐ The student used correct spelling and punctuation.

Notes:_____

2—Basic

☐ The student read the information with assistance from the teacher.

☐ The student completed the Venn diagram and the paragraph with teacher assistance.

☐ The student did not always use correct spelling or punctuation.

☐ The student should repeat this task until he or she is proficient.

Notes:_____

1—Below Basic

☐ The student could not read the information.

☐ The student did not complete the Venn diagram or the paragraph.

☐ The student should repeat this task until he or she is proficient.

Notes:_____

Volatile Volcanoes *(cont.)*

Teacher Scoring Guide for Student Task 2

Directions: Put check marks in all of the boxes that apply in a specific category. A place for writing notes is given following each category.

4—Advanced

- ☐ The student used a variety of sources to research volcanoes.
- ☐ The student wrote a research report about a specific volcano.
- ☐ In the report the student included the kind of volcano, its location, when it last erupted, a description of the eruption, and a description of the damage it caused.
- ☐ The student listed the sources that were used in his or her report.
- ☐ The student used correct spelling and punctuation.
- ☐ The student included at least 15 of the listed vocabulary words (see page 73) correctly in his or her report.

  Notes:_____

3—Proficient

- ☐ The student used a variety of sources to research volcanoes.
- ☐ The student wrote a research report about a specific volcano.
- ☐ In the report the student included the kind of volcano, its location, when it last erupted, a description of the eruption, and a description of the damage it caused.
- ☐ The student listed the sources that were used in his or her report.
- ☐ The student used correct spelling and punctuation.

  Notes:_____

2—Basic

- ☐ The student did not use a variety of sources to research volcanoes.
- ☐ The student wrote a report, but it was not about a specific volcano.
- ☐ The student left out several of the following points: the kind of volcano, its location, when it last erupted, a description of the eruption, and a description of the damage it caused.
- ☐ The student did not list the sources they used or the list was incomplete.
- ☐ The student did not always use correct spelling and punctuation.
- ☐ The student should repeat this task until he or she is proficient.

  Notes:_____

1—Below Basic

- ☐ The student did not complete the assignment.
- ☐ The student should repeat this task until he or she is proficient.

  Notes:_____

Bibliography

Fiction

Cole, Joanna. *The Magic School Bus Blows Its Top.* Scholastic, 1996.

Cole, Joanna. *The Magic School Bus Inside Earth.* Scholastic, 1987.

Kudlinski, Kathleen V. *Earthquake! The Story of Old San Francisco.* Puffin, 1995.

Nonfiction

Bolt, Bruce A. *Earthquakes and Geological Discovery.* Scientific American Library, Vol. 46, 1993.

Field, Nancy and Adele Schepige. *Discovering Earthquakes.* Dog-Eared Publications, 1995.

Hauser, Jill Frankel. *Super Science Concoctions.* Williamson Publishing, 1997.

Lauber, Patricia. *Volcano: The Eruption and Healing of Mount St. Helens.* Aladdin Publishing, 1986.

Levy, Matthys and Mario Salvadori. *Why Earth Quakes.* W. W. Norton & Company, 1997.

Mascher, Bernice. *Strange Science: Planet Earth.* Tom Doherty Associates, 1993.

Simon, Seymour. *Earthquakes.* Mulberry Books, 1995.

Steele, Phillip. *Rocking and Rolling.* Candlewick Press, 1997.

Books and CD-ROMS

Amundson, Burt. *Active Faults of San Francisco and Hollister.* Hopkins Technology, LLC. 1998.

World Book, Inc. *Volcanoes.* Two-Can Publishing Ltd., 1998.

Web Sites

ABCs of Earthquakes
http://edtech.kennesaw.edu/web/earthqu.html

Exploring Plate Tectonics
http://volcanoes.usgs.gov/Hazards/Where/WhereHaz.html

MTU Volcano Page
http://www.geo.mtu.edu/volcanoes/

Stromboli Volcano
http://educeth.ethz.ch/stromboli/

Volcano World
http://volcano.und.nodak.edu/

Volcano.com
http://volcanoes.com/

Volcanoes
http://volcano.und.nodak.edu/volcanoes.html

Answer Key

Page 22
1. b, c, d
2. a, d
3. b, c, d
4. b, c, d
5. a, d
6. a, b, d

Page 33

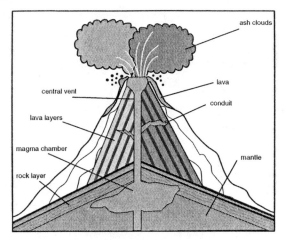

Page 34
1. 318 feet (97 m)
2. 5 miles (8 km) wide, 25 miles (40 km) wide
3. 2 feet (61 cm)
4. 300 square miles (777 square km)
5. 8,477 feet high (2,584 km)

Page 39

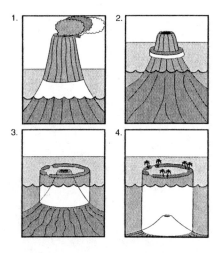

Page 44
1. Put a slice of white bread on a piece of aluminum foil.
2. Sprinkle a few drops of water on the bread.
3. Put the bread outside and leave it out overnight.
4. Put the bread in a plastic bag and seal it tightly.
5. Place the bag in a darkened area.
6. Use a magnifying glass to observe the bread in the bag. Record changes on your Journal Record.

Page 46
1. caldera
2. seismometer
3. volcanology
4. eruptions
5. magma
6. planets
7. Explosive
8. Pyroclastic
9. Mudflows
10. pumice

Page 47
1. .6 or 60%
2. .5 or 50%
3. .6 or 60%
4. .9 or 90%
5. .67 or 67%
6. Example: $13 \div 22 = 59\%$

Page 48
California

Eureka __50%__
Sacramento __59%__
San Francisco __67%__
Parkfield __90%__
San Bernardino __60%__
Los Angeles __60%__

Page 49
1. Parkfield, 90% probability
2. Eureka, 50% probability
3. California

Page 50
1. in 70 minutes at 3:05
2. about 20 times
3. 1 hour at 10:27
4. 100 minutes
5. approximately 7,508 times

Page 53
1. Cascades—Northwestern U. S.
   Sierra Nevada—Western U. S.
   Black Hills—North Central U. S.
   Appalachians—East Central U. S.
2. Cascades—volcanic mountains
3. Appalachians—fold mountains
4. Black Hills—dome mountains
5. Sierra Nevada—block mountains
6. Accept responses that reflect information presented on page 52.